DAN SATER'S

Mediterranean

HOME PLANS

INTRODUCING 65
SUPERB DESIGNS IN
NEW MEDITERRANEAN STYLE

A DESIGNS DIRECT PUBLISHING BOOK

Presented by

Sater Design
C O L L E C T I O N

The Sater Design Collection, Inc.
The Center at the Springs
25241 Elementary Way, Suite 201, Bonita Springs, FL 34135

Dan F. Sater, II — CEO and Author

Rickard Bailey — Editor-in-Chief

Jennifer Emmons — Editor

Amy Fullwiler — Contributing Editor

Matt McGarry — Contributing Editor

Clare Ulik — Contributing Editor

Dave Jenkins — Illustrator

Holzhauer — Contributing Illustrator

Diane J. Zwack — Creative Director/Art Director

Kim Campeau — Graphic Artist

Emily Sessa — Graphic Artist

CONTRIBUTING PHOTOGRAPHERS

Everett & Soulé, Tom Harper, Dan Forer, Joseph Lapeyra, Michael Lowry,

William Minarich, Kim Sargent, Bruce Schaeffer, Laurence Taylor,

Doug Thompson, Oscar Thompson and CJ Walker

Front Cover Photo: Dan Forer
Back Cover Photos: Michael Lowry, Laurence Taylor
Front Flap Photo: CJ Walker

Printed by: Toppan Printing Co., Hong Kong

First Printing: September 2005

10 9 8 7 6 5 4 3 2

ISBN softcover: 1-932553-10-X

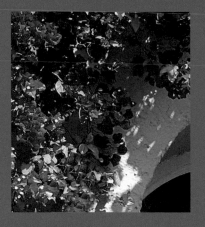

Contents

PHOTOGRAPH BY: CJ WALKER

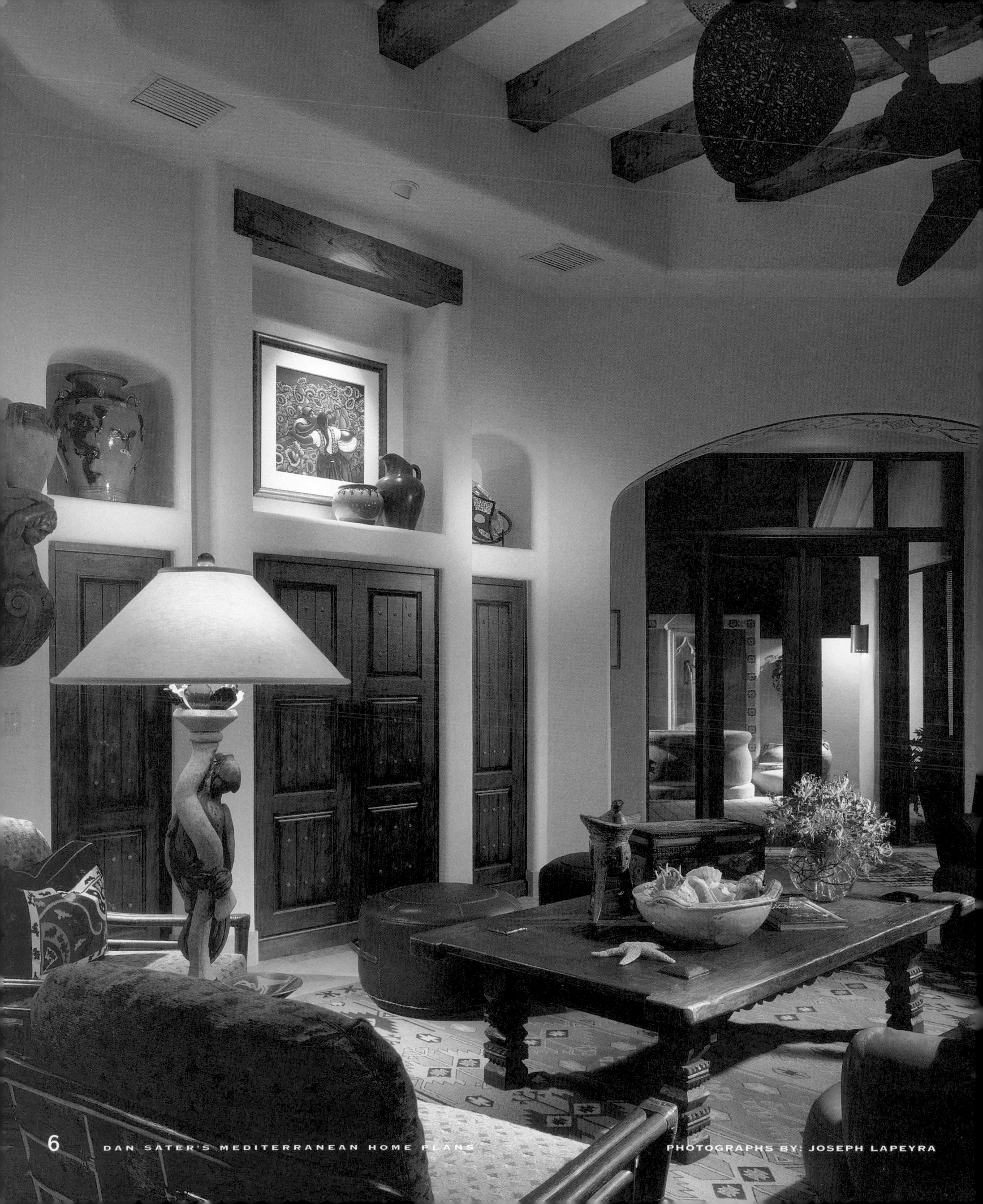

PHOTOGRAPHS BY: JOSEPH LAPEYRA

Design Philosophy

For critically acclaimed home designer Dan Sater, inspiration arrives in many forms: the gentle curve of a coastline, the texture of the trunk of a 100-year-old oak, the intense azure of a Florida sky. Motivation comes from deep within — a heartfelt desire to create homes that not only appeal to our deepest longing for easy and romantic lives, but that also meet the practical needs of the 21st-century family.

Mediterranean style offers Dan the perfect canvas for bringing his visions and eclectic ideas together in a home that leaves much to the imagination while leaving nothing out. He examines each design from many points of view, but first and foremost is his conceptual image of the future occupants. How they will live, work and play in the home provides the boundaries — the exterior walls, if you will — of each idea before it ever gets on paper.

Dan's earliest inspiration for Mediterranean design was the work of architect Addison Mizner (1872-1933) — a visionary who had no formal training yet is credited with creating the Spanish constitutions of Palm Beach and Boca Raton, and influencing the architectural flavor of many other Florida cities. Mizner once said his ambition was to "make a building look traditional and as though it had fought its way from a small unimportant structure to a great rambling house."

Similar is Dan Sater's ambition, seeking to blend Old World details — Moorish, Tuscan, Andalusian and Spanish — in a new, fresh way to create a home that both reflects history and reaches for the future. The look is simultaneously distinct and casual. Although Mediterranean design primarily is associated with tropical climates, Dan makes the style appealing to every corner of America. He achieves this with architectural amenities that relate to any outdoor environment, using large expanses of glass for viewing nature and wildlife, loggias and courtyards that harmonize indoor and outdoor living spaces, and pallets of organic colors and textures expressed throughout each room.

The Mediterranean Sea influences all of Southern Europe, embracing and impacting the coastlines of Spain, Italy and Greece. The architectural treasures of these countries eventually spilled over into Central and South America. Historically and architecturally rich, these regions

together offer a design treasure chest that Dan has drawn upon time and time again in creating homes with a cutting edge — sanctuaries for contemporary families who have genuine desires for homes with passion and personality coupled with modern-day needs for easy flow and high function.

In the end, Dan's success has been centered in his unparalleled ability to combine Old World details and textures with state-of-the-art ideas about design and function. The result is a "New" Mediterranean style that is uniquely his own and, ultimately, highly personal and comfortable for every family that builds a Sater home.

New Mediterranean Style

Like the multifaceted European and African coastlines and colorful Central American villages that inspired its creation, New Mediterranean design is dramatic and inviting, alive with texture and movement like a rolling ocean at sunset. The elements of new Mediterranean design have never been more beautifully showcased than in the photographs on the following pages.

Mediterranean style is actually an American vernacular. It originated in the early 1920s with legendary architect Addison Mizner, whose travels to Central America, Europe and even California served as the building blocks for his design ideas. Elite Northerners seeking to find their personal Eden in the mild climate of Florida's Atlantic coast embraced Mizner's vision: the style spoke to their hearts, and evoked fantasies of Old World elegance and a resort-like lifestyle that harmonized with nature and satisfied the inherent human need for warmth and comfort.

In architectural circles, Mediterranean refers to a blend of Spanish, Moorish and Tuscan influences borrowing in heritage from Romanesque-style architecture. The Spanish Colonial architecture of the New World was a precursor to the modern Mediterranean style. Intrinsic to the vernacular are such elements as stucco walls, arched or rounded vertical windows, and low-pitch, barrel-tile roofs. New Mediterranean style embraces all of these ancestral

ingredients and goes beyond to infuse the design with imprints of both past and future. For acclaimed home designer Dan Sater, this concept must include materials and features that reflect history and will last generations, as well as futuristic visions that fulfill the desires and demands of modern-day homeowners.

The possibilities of Mediterranean style are far-reaching and Dan routinely embraces details that are endlessly exciting: weathered stone, wood beams, rustic pavers, shaped corbels, ornamented arches and decorative tiles. All offer infinite potential for making each home ultimately unique. Soaring ceilings and disappearing glass walls blur the lines between traditional living spaces, and courtyards and solanas create niches with limitless promise for relaxing and entertaining.

A holistic approach is an absolute for Dan — thus he extends exterior façade details throughout the interior of the home to maintain purity in the design. The arches of the front windows are mirrored in the doorway opening. Rope columns flanking a turreted entryway show up between the breakfast bar and kitchen ceiling. The Spanish design and intricate tile work of a courtyard fireplace are mimicked in the hood and backsplash above the kitchen stove.

Each room maintains individuality. Foyers and living rooms are serene hosts to grand columns, soaring barrel-vaulted ceilings and stunning stone fireplaces. Master suites provide a perfect backdrop for whirlpool bathtubs, dramatic arched windows facing private gardens, and inlaid tray ceilings. Even the study — traditionally a utilitarian space for family business — becomes a work of art with richly carved and ornamented cabinetry.

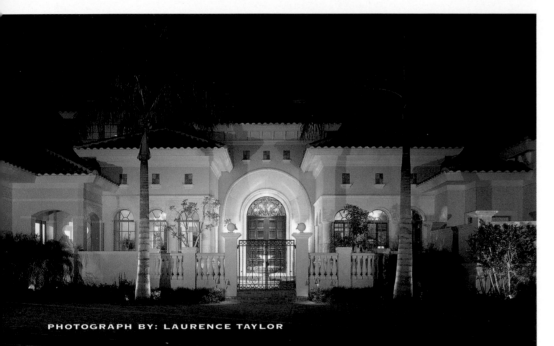

PHOTOGRAPH BY: LAURENCE TAYLOR

arched tops and shaped dormer windows.

In the Spanish eclectic vernacular, a home boasts a stucco façade, a tile roof, and a prominent arch over the entry doors and principal windows. Tuscan design supplies the almost fortress-like features of stone exteriors, sparse window openings, bracketed eaves, exposed rafter tails and rustic shutters.

Warm Mediterranean colors inject these design features with purity and personality. The red-gold of an ocean at sunset, the sienna of an Italian hillside and the burnt umber of a Spanish rooftop lend intrinsic warmth to the architecture and provide a wealth of interior design possibilities when choosing countertops, flooring, wall color and even furnishings and window dressings.

Texture is as important as hue, with varieties of stone, tile and ironwork adding dimension and individuality to features such as stove hoods, courtyard fireplaces, balcony railings and exterior window grills.

The warmth of the Mediterranean region implies that much time is spent outdoors, and spaces that offer alfresco living are a hallmark of every Sater-designed home. Rambling verandas and loggias are punctuated by Tuscan columns and arched framework to lend an air of exotic, resort-style living. Covered loggias have Spanish-inspired corner fireplaces and tiled flooring, as well as fully equipped kitchens that create unlimited outdoor entertainment venues. Richly appointed courtyards differ from comfortable, indoor leisure rooms only in their open ceilings — providing vast opportunities for intimate relaxing and visiting in a fresh-air environment.

Dan draws upon a wealth of architectural "themes" when designing a New Mediterranean home. Italian renaissance style suggests low-pitched hipped roofs, a symmetrical façade and entryways accented by columns or pilasters. Mission influences contribute porches with

The warmth of wood is found in door and window frames, cabinetry, moldings and ceiling beams — supplying another voice of nature in its rich organic contrast to smoothly textured walls, gently curving ceilings and sleek porcelain tiles.

From this bountiful mix of materials, textures and forms, Dan selects just the right elements — and applies his artist's eye and vision — to create an impeccable design that is perfect for many natural settings and environments. The result of 20 years of experience in working and refining this process yields some of the most fabulous Mediterranean-influenced home plans available today. Unlimited in possibilities and awash in fabulous architectural options, Dan Sater's New Mediterranean designs promise homes that are fluid and energizing, and as individual as their owners.

PHOTOGRAPH BY: LAURENCE TAYLOR

PHOTO ABOVE: *All angles, arches and sun-reflecting stucco, this home exudes the allure inherent in traditional Mediterranean design. Upper deck rooflines curve gracefully, their Spanish-inspired horseshoe lines seeming to mimic the waves of the sea they were originally created to complement. Custom home.*

PHOTO RIGHT: *A beamed, coffered ceiling and dramatic lighting add elegance to this has-it-all kitchen. Mediterranean influences are revealed in the custom hood, tiled backsplash and cabinetry arches, while modern efficiencies are exemplified in the furniture-style, butcher-block island and gleaming commercial range. Plan 6942, page 22.*

PHOTOGRAPH BY: JOSEPH LAPEYRA

PHOTOGRAPH BY: JOSEPH LAPEYRA

PHOTO ABOVE: *A puckered arch defines the passageway from the leisure room to kitchen, and an octagonal-shaped, tongue-and-groove cypress ceiling adds an organic element to this family area.*

Plan 6942, page 22.

Elements of Design

PHOTO LEFT: *Oversized Moorish, rough-hewn wood doors leading to a wine cooler wear iron hardware that provides a weighty, Old World element. The texture provides sturdy contrast to the gracefully carved arches of the doorways, the soft hues of the walls and the intricate tile design. Plan 6942, page 22.*

PHOTO TOP RIGHT: *Rough wood ceiling beams and soft lights guide passage down a hall that ends in a dramatic art niche. To either side of the niche are guest suites, and midway down the hall is access to the kitchen on one side and a walk-in pantry on the other. Plan 6947, page 30.*

PHOTO BOTTOM RIGHT: *Textured sienna walls provide a stunning backdrop for a dramatic vanity in a secondary bathroom. The organic materials of the counter area and floor contrast with a contemporary glass bowl, giving this bath a true New Mediterranean flavor. Plan 6947, page 30.*

PHOTO BOTTOM LEFT: *Distinct in design, this octagonal-shaped courtyard tucked into a corner of the lanai offers Spanish flavor in the fireplace and stove hood. Proximity to the leisure room makes this cozy space perfect for everyday dining. Plan 6947, page 30.*

Elements of Design

This charming Mediterranean home freely blends a mixture of shapes and textures. Tall, narrow, arch-topped windows alongside Moorish-shaped niches are punctuated by roofline corbels and decorative wrought-iron grillwork. Plan 6932, page 62.

PHOTOGRAPH BY: JOSEPH LAPEYRA

PHOTO ABOVE: *An angled ceiling tray and the varying doorway arches add flair to this spectacular master suite. A magnificent sitting room is embraced by quadruple bay windows, which view the pool area beyond. Plan 6942, page 22.*

Elements of Design

PHOTOGRAPH BY: CJ WALKER

PHOTO ABOVE: *Varnished wood beams float beneath a beadboard ceiling, providing intimacy to this expansive yet ultra-functional kitchen. Mediterranean influences abound, from the sleek bar columns and custom tiled backsplash to the Spanish-influenced stove hood. Custom home.*

PHOTO RIGHT: *Custom cabinetry and a granite countertop offer limitless storage and additional workspace adjacent to a gleaming kitchen. A second door leading to additional storage spaces and a utility room give this butler's pantry a multipurpose focus. Plan 6935, page 36.*

PHOTOGRAPH BY: JOSEPH LAPEYRA

PHOTO ABOVE: *Circular detailing and honey-colored organic materials infuse this master bath with sophistication and luxury. This Roman tub provides the perfect vantage point for a relaxing view of the master garden. Custom home.*

Elements of Design

PHOTO ABOVE: *Rustic beams add texture and soften the passage from bedroom to sitting room. This oversized master suite encompasses one entire side of the home and features stepped ceilings, a washer/dryer in one of the two walk-in closets, and French doors to the lanai. Plan 6947, page 30.*

PHOTO ABOVE: *Dappled sunlight fills this charming courtyard, pooling around a center fountain ringed by color-laden plants. A massive stone and wrought-iron entry sets the tone for the impressive home beyond this purely Mediterranean terrace. Plan 6935, page 36.*

PHOTO RIGHT: *A hand-painted domed ceiling plays host to a tiered candelabra, and a ring of medallions casts sophistication upon the gallery and staircase. Wrought-iron detailing is further carried through the home in the stair rail, which flows gracefully from a spectacular first-floor foyer. Plan 6935, page 36.*

Marrakesh

PHOTOGRAPHY BY: JOSEPH LAPEYRA

PHOTO ABOVE: *Like a cool, blue pool in a sandy desert, this Spanish Colonial Revival villa is the centerpiece of an oasis of its own creation, capturing mystery, beauty and enchantment.*

PHOTO RIGHT: *There's no lack in this has-it-all kitchen. The furniture-style, butcher-block island and gleaming commercial range lend first-class efficiency, while the beamed coffered ceiling and dramatic lighting add flair.*

PHOTO FAR RIGHT: *A curving wall of three soaring, pointed-arch windows opens the living room to the patio beyond.*

PHOTO ABOVE: Pointed-arch windows with delicate framework make for elegant outdoor viewing from a comfortable dining room. A mirrored buffet boasts dramatic carvings and corbels, and softly hued walls emit all the warmth needed for memorable meals.

PHOTO RIGHT: A puckered arch defines the passageway from leisure room to kitchen, and a custom-appointed serving bar provides a perfect spot for the components of a casual buffet or intimate conversation with the cook.

PHOTO ABOVE: *A spectacular master suite occupies one side of the home. An angled bedroom with a tray ceiling features headboard and art niches along with a magnificent sitting room embraced by a quadruple bay window.*

PHOTO LEFT: *A series of pillared arches nobly lead to the master bath. An oval tub is dramatically centered under a coffered ceiling and faces a private garden through bay windows.*

PHOTO ABOVE: *The multiple angles and curves of the rear façade create unique niches, such as this one for plein-air dining. Columns and arched rooflines frame the patio with Mediterranean detail.*

PHOTO RIGHT: *Lanai profiles mimic and draw attention to the pointed-arch living room window, while a secluded nook created by angled walls of glass offers an ideal spot for a morning latte.*

PHOTO ABOVE: *An exposed-beam ceiling in the solana gives the space a rustic feel. On cool evenings, the tiled, outdoor hearth offers a perfect gathering spot for intimate talks or a late-night snack.*

PHOTO TOP LEFT: *Entrancing walls and a furniture-style vanity topped by an ornately carved mirror give a sense of opulence to a powder room conveniently tucked between the living and leisure rooms.*

PHOTO LEFT: *This feature-laden wet bar is elegantly appointed and perfectly placed near the wine cooler, living, dining and kitchen areas.*

PHOTO ABOVE: *A freestanding whirlpool tub encased in natural stone and marble takes center stage in a truly dramatic master bath. The pointed-arch windows connect this opulent bath to a private garden, and expanded custom vanities provide an abundance of storage and pampering amenities.*

PHOTO RIGHT: *Tile-framed, arched mirrors under a fifteen-foot, coffered ceiling expand this striking bath and offer multiple reflections of the lush privacy garden.*

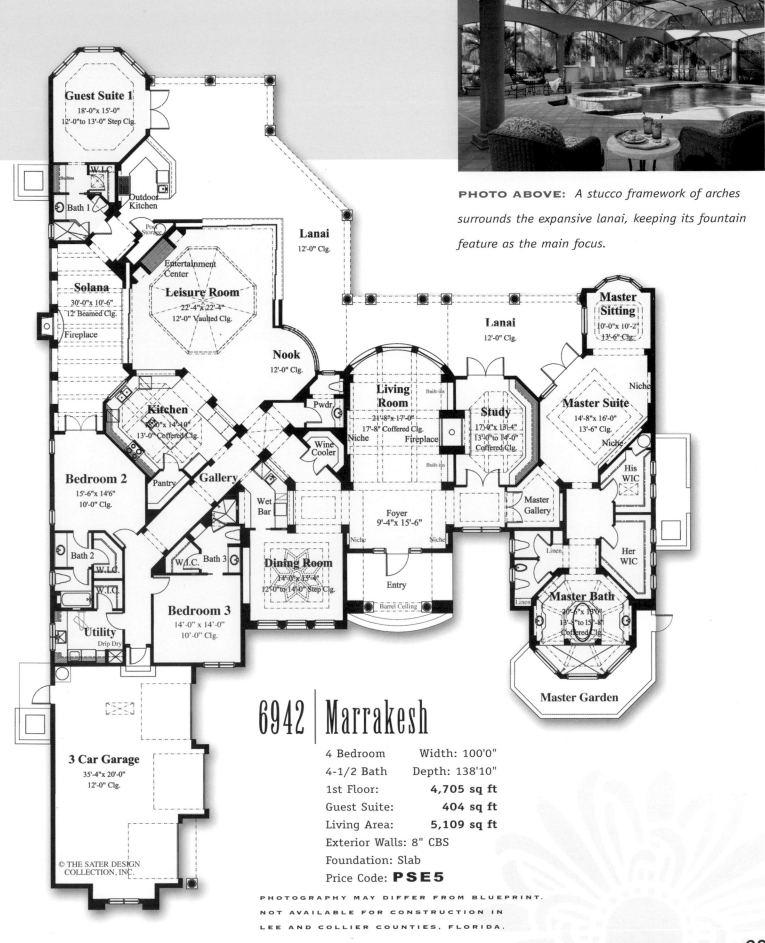

Guest Suite 1
18'-0"x 15'-0"
12'-0"to 13'-0" Step Clg.

W.I.C.

Builtins

Bath 1

Outdoor Kitchen

Pool Storage

Lanai
12'-0" Clg.

Entertainment Center

Solana
30'-0"x 10'-6"
12' Beamed Clg.

Fireplace

Leisure Room
22'-4"x 22'-4"
12'-0" Vaulted Clg.

Nook
12'-0" Clg.

Lanai
12'-0" Clg.

Master Sitting
10'-0"x 10'-2"
13'-6" Clg.

Niche

Living Room
21'-8"x 17'-0"
17'-8" Coffered Clg.

Built-ins

Study
17'-0"x 13'-4"
13'-0" to 14'-0"
Coffered Clg.

Master Suite
14'-8"x 16'-0"
13'-6" Clg.

Niche

Kitchen
13'-0"x 14'-10"
13'-0" Coffered Clg.

Pwdr.

Niche

Fireplace

Built-ins

Niche

His WIC

Wine Cooler

Bedroom 2
15'-6"x 14'6"
10'-0" Clg.

Pantry

Gallery

Wet Bar

Master Gallery

Linen

Her WIC

Bath 2

W.I.C.

W.I.C.

Bath 3

Foyer
9'-4"x 15'-6"

Niche

Niche

Utility
Drip Dry

Bedroom 3
14'-0" x 14'-0"
10'-0" Clg.

Dining Room
14'-0"x 13'-4"
12'-0" to 14'-0" Step Clg.

Entry

Barrel Ceiling

Master Bath
20'-6"x 13'-0"
13'-8" to 15'-8"
Coffered Clg.

Linen

3 Car Garage
35'-4"x 20'-0"
12'-0" Clg.

Master Garden

6942 | Marrakesh

4 Bedroom	Width: 100'0"
4-1/2 Bath	Depth: 138'10"
1st Floor:	**4,705 sq ft**
Guest Suite:	**404 sq ft**
Living Area:	**5,109 sq ft**

Exterior Walls: 8" CBS

Foundation: Slab

Price Code: **PSE5**

PHOTO ABOVE: A stucco framework of arches surrounds the expansive lanai, keeping its fountain feature as the main focus.

Sancho

PHOTOGRAPHY BY: JOSEPH LAPEYRA

PHOTO ABOVE: *The influence of Spanish style is clearly evident in this rambling home that truly welcomes the outside in. Lush planters greet visitors as they enter an engaging entry turret made even grander by a decorative, second-story, wrought-iron balcony. Further accenting the great outdoors is an expansive covered loggia that wraps the rear elevation.*

PHOTO RIGHT: *Optional "his" and "hers" studies feature beautiful, custom-wood built-ins and access to the loggia through double doors.*

PHOTO FAR RIGHT: *Wrought-iron accents and rough-hewn wood bring a rustic elegance to this grand foyer.*

Sancho

PHOTO ABOVE: *A charming chimenea-style fireplace warms the outdoor kitchen and adjacent sitting area. An extended serving counter makes for perfect buffets — and conversations.*

PHOTO RIGHT: *An entrancing powder room, conveniently located across the hall from the wet bar, exemplifies the charm of Mediterranean design.*

PHOTO ABOVE: *With spacious swirled granite counters, ample cabinet storage space, and a convenient butcher-block center island under a wrought-iron pot rack, this octagonal gourmet kitchen is friendly to chefs, family and friends alike.*

PHOTO LEFT: *A work of art in itself, an elegant art niche at the entrance of the guest suite provides the perfect home for a favorite painting or sculpture.*

PHOTO ABOVE: *Occupying the entire left side of the floor plan, the master suite is incredibly spacious yet private. This retreat boasts "his" and "hers" walk-in closets and studies, a sitting area, and an elegant master bedroom – seen here – with access to the loggia through sliding glass doors.*

PHOTO RIGHT: *Graceful arches and golden hues give this opulent master bath its air of lavish comfort. Reflected in the arch-top vanity mirror is a window seat that overlooks the home's privacy garden.*

PHOTO TOP RIGHT: *Adjoining the leisure and guest rooms is a butterfly garden — the perfect spot for a sunny afternoon.*

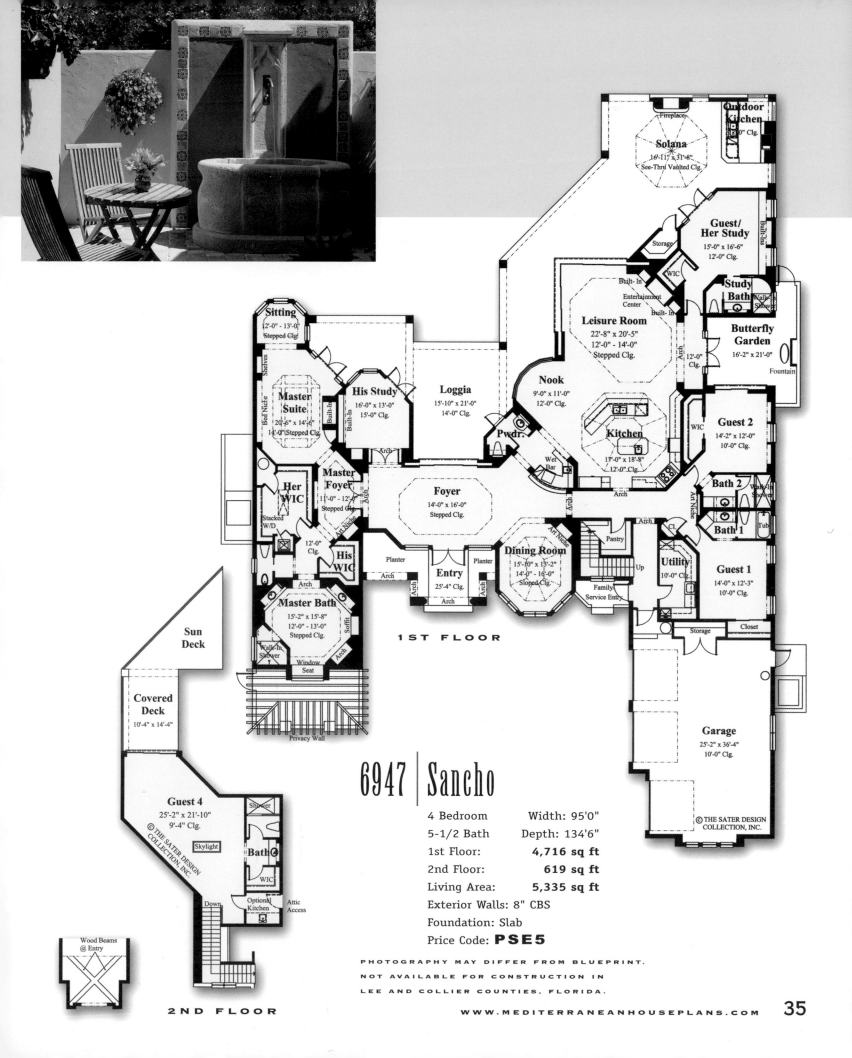

1ST FLOOR

Solana
16'-11" x 31'-8"
See-Thru Vaulted Clg.

Outdoor Kitchen

Guest/ Her Study
15'-0" x 16'-6"
12'-0" Clg.

Storage

WIC

Built-In Entertainment Center

Study Bath

Leisure Room
22'-8" x 20'-5"
12'-0" - 14'-0"
Stepped Clg.

Butterfly Garden
16'-2" x 21'-0"
Fountain

Sitting
12'-0" - 13'-0"
Stepped Clg.

His Study
16'-0" x 13'-0"
15'-0" Clg.

Loggia
15'-10" x 21'-0"
14'-0" Clg.

Nook
9'-0" x 11'-0"
12'-0" Clg.

Kitchen
17'-0" x 18'-8"
12'-0" Clg.

Guest 2
14'-2" x 12'-0"
10'-0" Clg.

Master Suite
20'-6" x 14'-6"
14'-0" Stepped Clg.

Master Foyer
11'-0" - 12'-8"
Stepped Clg.

Her WIC

Pwdr.

Wet Bar

WIC

Bath 2

His WIC

Foyer
14'-0" x 16'-0"
Stepped Clg.

Pantry

Bath 1

Planter

Entry
25'-4" Clg.

Planter

Dining Room
15'-10" x 13'-2"
14'-0" - 16'-0"
Sloped Clg.

Up

Utility
10'-0" Clg.

Guest 1
14'-0" x 12'-3"
10'-0" Clg.

Master Bath
15'-2" x 15'-8"
12'-0" - 13'-0"
Stepped Clg.

Walk-In Shower

Window Seat

Privacy Wall

Family Service Entry

Storage

Closet

Garage
25'-2" x 36'-4"
10'-0" Clg.

© THE SATER DESIGN COLLECTION, INC.

2ND FLOOR

Sun Deck

Covered Deck
10'-4" x 14'-4"

Guest 4
25'-2" x 21'-10"
9'-4" Clg.

Shower

Skylight

Bath

WIC

Down

Optional Kitchen

Attic Access

© THE SATER DESIGN COLLECTION, INC.

Wood Beams @ Entry

6947 | Sancho

4 Bedroom   Width: 95'0"

5-1/2 Bath   Depth: 134'6"

1st Floor: **4,716 sq ft**

2nd Floor: **619 sq ft**

Living Area: **5,335 sq ft**

Exterior Walls: 8" CBS

Foundation: Slab

Price Code: **PSE5**

Casa Bellisima

PHOTOGRAPHY BY: JOSEPH LAPEYRA

PHOTO ABOVE: *A cast-stone, arched entry commands a stunning focal point at the front of this pure Mediterranean home.*

PHOTO RIGHT: *Stone steps, scrolling wrought iron, cast-stone ornamentals, dentil molding and a magnificent cupola add captivating details to the entry and front façade.*

PHOTO FAR RIGHT: *An elegant spiral staircase leads from the striking circular gallery to a loft and guest suite. Just beyond, perfectly located between the butler's pantry and wet bar, is the well-stocked wine cellar.*

PHOTO ABOVE: *An angled bar and center island provide necessary amenities for this family-oriented kitchen. Notice how the uniquely tiled backsplash and stove hood play off the warm cabinetry and wood-beamed tray ceiling.*

PHOTO RIGHT: *A dramatic foyer offers elegant entrance to the study and master suite. French doors lead to the study, while double doors open to the master suite.*

PHOTO FAR RIGHT: *A spectacular floor-to-ceiling fireplace and surrounding display niches create high drama in the living room.*

PHOTO ABOVE: *A game room loft features a coffered ceiling and art displays. Architectural details such as arches and columns add sophistication, while a full-service wet bar blends with play spaces to make this a flexible chamber with varied uses.*

PHOTO RIGHT: *A custom, corner entertainment center in the leisure room provides focus under a diamond-shaped, wood-beamed ceiling. Disappearing sliding glass walls merge two sides of the room with the veranda for seamless indoor-outdoor flow. An elliptical-shaped nook bridges the room and the adjacent kitchen.*

PHOTO ABOVE: *A massive veranda feels like an elegant outdoor room, bursting with dramatic ambience. Stucco arches are repeated around the perimeter. An intricate-shaped pool plays center stage to a gentle water feature. An outdoor kitchen and fireplace off the leisure room make this exhilarating space livable year-round.*

PHOTO LEFT: *A three-sided fireplace with hand-painted chimney offers charming punctuation between the diamond-shaped master suite and an accompanying sitting room. Other features include an intricately detailed coffered ceiling, and a foyer offering access to two walk-in closets and a dressing area.*

PHOTO ABOVE: *A striking fireplace framed by copper-colored tiles and mantle creates a longing for intimacy in a cozy corner of the veranda. Nearby, a custom-designed stone table offers limitless dining options for friend-filled Sunday brunches and one-on-one sunset dinners.*

PHOTO RIGHT: *Rich custom cabinetry and intricate wood-framed windows give the study classic tendencies worthy of a grand estate. Located to the right of the entry and just off the master-suite foyer, the study offers a coffered ceiling and front courtyard views.*

2ND FLOOR

Guest Suite
23'-3" x 14'-0"
10'-0" to 10'-8"
Stepped Clg.

Deck

W.I.C.
Walk-In Shower

Guest Bath

Mech. Room

Wet Bar
11'-0" to 12'-0"
Stepped Clg.

Game Room / Loft
29'-0" x 28'-1"
11'-0" to 12'-0" Coffered Clg.

© THE SATER DESIGN COLLECTION, INC.

Open to Below
21'-0" to 22'-0"
Coffered Clg.

Up

Dn.

1ST FLOOR

Planter

Pool Deck

Kiddie Pool

Pool Deck

Veranda
11'-6" Clg.

Pool

Pool Shower

Fireplace

Outdoor Kitchen
11'-6" Clg.

Leisure Room
21'-9" x 21'-9"
Vaulted Clg.

Entertainment Center

Planter

Spa

Planter

Sitting
16'-0" to 16'-8"
Stepped Clg.

Courtyard

Nook
10'-6" Clg.

Veranda
11'-6" Clg.

Veranda
13'-0" Clg.

Pool Bath
10'-3" Clg.

3-Sided Fireplace

Living Room
20'-6" x 18'-0"
Open to Above

Fireplace

Walk-In Shower

Master Suite
27'-0" x 15'-1"
13'-0" to 14'-4"
Coffered Clg.

Kitchen
18'-0" x 17'-0"
10'-6" to 11'-6" Clg.

Wet Bar

Wine Cellar

Gallery

Up

Powder Bath

Niche

Master Foyer
12'-0" to 13'-0"
Stepped Clg.

Art Niche

W.I.C.

Butler Pantry
10'-6" Clg.

Guest Suite 1
16'-0" x 14'-8"
11'-6" Clg.

W.I.C.

Storage

Foyer
Barrel Vault Clg.

W.I.C.

Dressing Area

Walk-In Shower

Gallery
10'-6" Clg.

Dining Room
17'-7" x 16'-2"
15'-0" to 16'-6"
Beamed Clg.

Utility
10'-0" Clg.

Entry
Barrel Vault Clg.

Storage

Study
18'-3" x 14'-10"
14'-0" to 15'-0"
Coffered Clg.

Master Bath

Make-up Area

Guest Bath 1

Walk-In Shower

W.I.C.

Guest Bath 2

Service Entrance

Courtyard

Fountain

Whirlpool

Walk-In Shower

Guest Suite 2
15'-8" x 13'-8"
11'-6" Clg.

Storage

Master Garden

Garage
39'-2" x 24'-8"
15'-0" Clg.

© THE SATER DESIGN COLLECTION, INC.

6935 | Casa Bellisima

4 Bedroom   Width: 104'0"
5-1/2 Bath   Depth: 140'0"
1st Floor: **5,391 sq ft**
2nd Floor: **1,133 sq ft**
Living Area: **6,524 sq ft**
Exterior Walls: 8" CBS
Foundation: Slab
Price Code: **PSE5**

PHOTO ABOVE: *The music of multiple waterfalls accompanies every meal savored on this veranda.*

PHOTO ABOVE: *Dramatic stained-glass divides the floating bathtub from a hidden steam room.*

Lindley

PHOTOGRAPHY BY: LAURENCE TAYLOR

PHOTO ABOVE: *Graceful Renaissance lines inspired by captivating, rural European villas create a street presence of extraordinary beauty with this sun-country estate. Sculpted recesses draw the eye toward the formal entry, capped by a stunning fanlight.*

PHOTO RIGHT: *A row of transoms borders the stepped ceiling of the living room, which is defined by a massive fireplace with a carved mantel and a rusticated stone surround.*

PHOTO FAR RIGHT: *A colonnade of tall, arch-top windows grants extensive views of the entry court and front property.*

PHOTO ABOVE: *The gourmet kitchen mixes a timber-beamed ceiling, a sculpted stove hood and marble countertops in a rustic European motif that evokes the charm of a Mediterranean villa. A framed mural above the stove echoes the rich accent colors in the countertops.*

PHOTO ABOVE: *Unexpected architecture creates seamless boundaries between a koi pond bordered with lush planters and outdoor living spaces, which include an alfresco dining area. An elaborated chimney-top signals a European provenance.*

PHOTO ABOVE: *Buttercream walls offer depth and dimension to the leisure room, with views that telescope through a covered lanai and the pool area to the great outdoors. A pyramid ceiling, sculpted recesses and built-in niches and cabinetry add texture to the arena.*

PHOTO LEFT: *Pilasters and rope columns create a stunning pass-through between the leisure room and kitchen. Double doors open to a serene courtyard.*

PHOTO ABOVE: *Pillars, arches and a continuous floor visually connect the leisure room, kitchen and dining nook. A custom buffet set in an arched niche beautifully serves to unify and enhance this ideal gathering space.*

PHOTO RIGHT: *Rope columns frame the entry to the living room, enhanced by natural light and deep views through a wall of paneled glass. Transoms top the space with wrought-iron details that complement the ornate lighting fixture above the entry.*

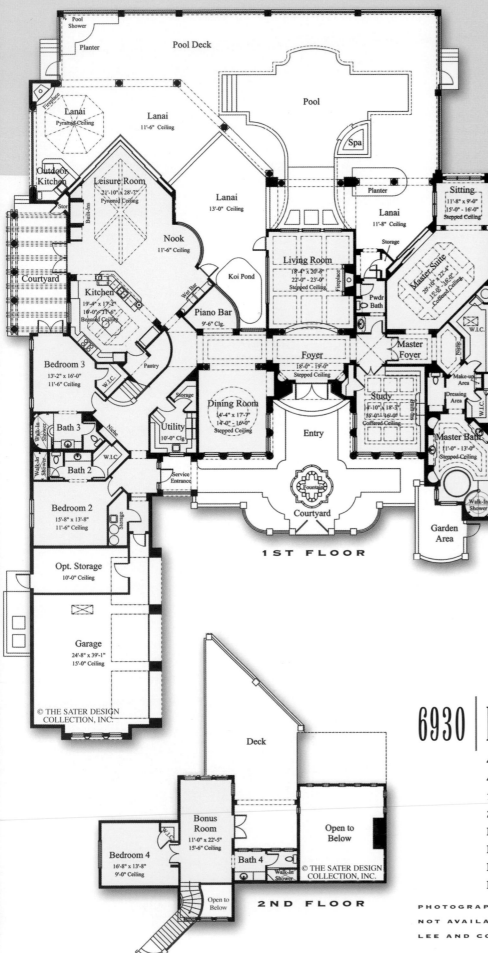

1ST FLOOR

Pool Shower
Planter
Pool Deck
Lanai (Pyramid Ceiling)
Lanai 11'-6" Ceiling
Pool
Spa
Fireplace
Outdoor Kitchen
Lanai 13'-0" Ceiling
Planter
Sitting 11'-8" x 9'-0" 15'-0" x 16'-0" Stepped Ceiling
Leisure Room 21'-10" x 28'-7" Pyramid Ceiling
Courtyard
Nook 11'-6" Ceiling
Koi Pond
Living Room 18'-4" x 20'-8" 22'-0" - 23'-0" Stepped Ceiling
Lanai 11'-8" Ceiling
Storage
Master Suite 20'-10" x 22'-6" 15'-0" - 16'-0" Coffered Ceiling
Kitchen 19'-4" x 17'-2" 10'-0"-11'-6" Beamed Ceiling
Wet Bar
Piano Bar 9'-6" Clg.
Fireplace
Pwdr Bath
W.I.C.
Bedroom 3 13'-2" x 16'-0" 11'-6" Ceiling
Pantry
Foyer 18'-0" - 19'-0" Stepped Ceiling
Master Foyer
Make-up Area
Storage
W.I.C.
Bath 3
Storage
Dining Room 14'-4" x 17'-7" 14'-0" - 16'-0" Stepped Ceiling
Utility 10'-0" Clg.
Study 14'-10" x 18'-3" 15'-0" - 16'-0" Coffered Ceiling
Dressing Area
Walk-In Shower
Niche
W.I.C.
Bath 2
Entry
Master Bath 11'-0" - 13'-0" Stepped Ceiling
Walk-In Shower
Service Entrance
Bedroom 2 15'-8" x 13'-8" 11'-6" Ceiling
Storage
Fountain
Courtyard
Walk-In Shower
Opt. Storage 10'-0" Ceiling
Garden Area
Garage 24'-8" x 39'-1" 15'-0" Ceiling

© THE SATER DESIGN COLLECTION, INC.

2ND FLOOR

Deck
Bonus Room 11'-0" x 22'-5" 15'-6" Ceiling
Open to Below
Bedroom 4 16'-8" x 13'-8" 9'-0" Ceiling
Bath 4
Walk-In Shower
Open to Below
Open to Below

© THE SATER DESIGN COLLECTION, INC.

PHOTO ABOVE: *A spacious master suite seamlessly blends a room-sized sitting space with a bounty of views and access to a private lanai.*

PHOTO ABOVE: *An art niche and sculpture add an air of repose to this open master bath. A vintage chaise lounge helps amplify the sense of luxury created by a step-down shower and spa-style tub.*

6930 | Lindley

4 Bedroom	Width: 99'4"
4-1/2 Bath	Depth: 140'0"
1st Floor:	**5,265 sq ft**
2nd Floor:	**746 sq ft**
Living Area:	**6,011 sq ft**
Exterior Walls:	8" CBS
Foundation:	Slab
Price Code:	**PSE5**

Fiorentino

PHOTOGRAPHY BY: DAN FORER

PHOTO ABOVE: *This aristocratic country villa could have been transported from a hillside in northern Italy. The softness of the low-pitch roofs, in juxtaposition to the magnificent rotunda that dominates the front elevation, gives the entrance an aura of serene elegance.*

PHOTO RIGHT: *The handsome leisure room is spacious and warm, featuring a corner fireplace, built-in entertainment center, exposed-beam ceiling and zero-corner sliding glass doors.*

PHOTO FAR RIGHT: *This Italianate-style rotunda staircase neatly carves out an ample wine cellar.*

PHOTO ABOVE: *Rich accents in wood bring an aura of Old World grace and sophistication to a private study adjacent to the formal living room.*

PHOTO RIGHT: *The emphasis might appear to be more on form than function, but don't be deceived — this picture-perfect kitchen is deceptively hard-working. Enjoying ample space for a professional-grade hooded range, double sinks and spacious dual pantries, the chef of this home could easily manage a dinner party for twelve.*

PHOTO ABOVE: *A breezy, rambling loggia wraps the rear elevation. Decorative columns and pillars gracefully bear a beautiful burden — the weight of a second-story observation deck that opens into the starry sky above.*

PHOTO LEFT: *A spectacular breakfast nook encased in circular glass offers dramatic daytime dining. The columns of the loggia roof stand like sentries at a luxurious resort.*

PHOTO ABOVE: *With its soaring, twenty-foot vaulted ceiling, towering Ionic columns and graceful arches, this superbly spacious rotunda living area is, without a doubt, the heart and soul of the home.*

PHOTO RIGHT: *The master suite is truly a crown jewel in this opulent home design, with a sitting area that opens to the loggia via glass doors.*

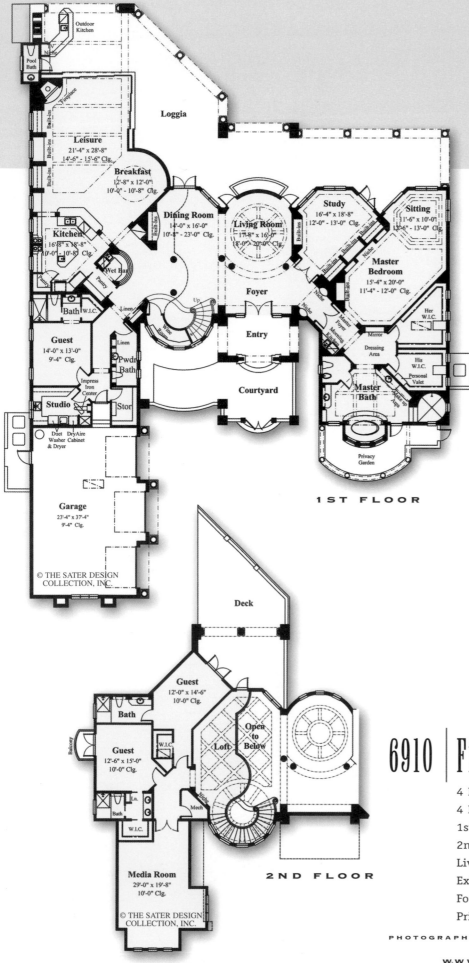

1ST FLOOR

Outdoor Kitchen

Pool Bath

Loggia

Leisure
21'-4" x 28'-8"
14'-6" - 15'-6" Clg.

Built-ins

Fireplace

Breakfast
12'-8" x 12'-0"
10'-0" - 10'-8" Clg.

Dining Room
14'-0" x 16'-0"
10'-8" - 23'-0" Clg.

Kitchen
16'-8" x 18'-8"
10'-0" - 10'-8" Clg.

Wet Bar

Pantry

Living Room
17'-8" x 16'-0"
18'-0" x 20'-0" Clg.

Study
16'-4" x 18'-8"
12'-0" - 13'-0" Clg.

Sitting
11'-6" x 10'-0"
12'-6" - 13'-0" Clg.

Foyer

Master Bedroom
15'-4" x 20'-0"
11'-4" - 12'-0" Clg.

Her W.I.C.

Bath

W.I.C.

Linen

Guest
14'-0" x 13'-0"
9'-4" Clg.

Linen

Wine Room

Up

Pwdr Bath

Entry

Mirror

Master Foyer

Dressing Area

His W.I.C.

Personal Valet

Make up Area

Impress Iron Center

Studio

Stor

Courtyard

Master Bath

Duet DryAire Washer Cabinet & Dryer

Privacy Garden

Garage
23'-4" x 37'-4"
9'-4" Clg.

© THE SATER DESIGN COLLECTION, INC.

2ND FLOOR

Deck

Guest
12'-0" x 14'-6"
10'-0" Clg.

Bath

Guest
12'-6" x 15'-0"
10'-0" Clg.

Balcony

W.I.C.

Open to Below

Loft

Bath

Ln.

W.I.C.

Mech

Media Room
29'-0" x 19'-8"
10'-0" Clg.

© THE SATER DESIGN COLLECTION, INC.

PHOTO ABOVE: *The loft above the dining area is defined by an ornate, wrought-iron railing.*

PHOTO ABOVE: *An elevated garden tub in the master suite overlooks the privacy garden.*

6910 | Fiorentino

4 Bedroom	Width: 96'0"
4 Full, 2 Half Baths	Depth: 134'8"
1st Floor:	**4,742 sq ft**
2nd Floor:	**1,531 sq ft**
Living Area:	**6,273 sq ft**

Exterior Walls: 8" CBS

Foundation: Slab

Price Code: **PSE5**

PHOTOGRAPHY MAY DIFFER FROM BLUEPRINT.

Ristano

PHOTOGRAPHY BY: MICHAEL LOWRY

PHOTO ABOVE: *Snow-white window trim gives a storybook quality to this elegant Mediterranean manor, where repeated use of narrow vertical windows enhances an elevation that stretches skyward and focuses attention on a dramatic vaulted entryway.*

PHOTO RIGHT: *A corner wet bar serves multiple purposes by providing easy access to entertaining for the dining and living rooms as well as the kitchen.*

PHOTO FAR RIGHT: *Stone columns make a glorious framework for viewing a sheer wall of curved glass that defines the living room.*

PHOTO ABOVE: Nestled into one end of the veranda, the master suite exudes elegant respite. An embracing arch leads the way into a cozy sitting area that offers stirring views through a series of vertical windows. Private access to the back patios, a spectacular bathroom and a large morning kitchen complement this refined retreat.

PHOTO RIGHT: A spa-style tub encased in wood and marble floats before a glass door leading to a private garden. A walk-in shower is encased in intensely hued natural materials and a curved glass wall, and an arched mirror over the vanity expands the space and magnifies the opulence.

PHOTO ABOVE: A customized wall of niches provides space for artwork, a media center, an angled fireplace and a cozy window seat in the leisure room. Sliding glass walls extend the space into the outdoor kitchen to the right and the interior kitchen to the left.

PHOTO LEFT: Flowing smoothly into the expansive leisure room and a glass-walled breakfast nook, the kitchen offers a plethora of amenities in a functional configuration. A center island includes lots of storage and a sink, and cabinetry is plentiful.

PHOTO ABOVE: *Magnificent lines indicate unlimited possibilities for daily living as well as grand entertaining. A corbelled roofline and upper deck framed in wrought iron extend the home out and upward, while the multi-angled veranda follows the curves and corners of interesting rooms and a free-form pool, providing a myriad of outdoor-embracing niches.*

PHOTO RIGHT: *An open flow defines the dining room, utilizing sleek columns and a stepped ceiling to accentuate its height, and an opulent floor pattern and enchanting chandelier to profess glamour. Easy access to a wine cellar and a wet bar add to the luxury.*

PHOTO ABOVE: *A gently curved glass window frames the living room and entry foyer, sending a message that these spaces are truly works of art.*

1ST FLOOR

Outdoor Grille

Outdoor Kitchen
8'-10" x 9'-8"
Open to Above

Outdoor Fireplace

Pool Stor.

Fireplace

Leisure
20'-0" x 21'-0"
Open to Above

Built-In Entertainment Center

Built-In Window Seat

Veranda
12'-0" Clg.

Nook
12'-0" Clg.

Pool Bath
12'-0" Clg.

Veranda
16'-0" Clg.

Veranda
13'-8" Clg.

Sitting Area
10'-8" to 12'-0" Tray Clg.

Kitchen
21'-5" x 16'-8"
11'-4" To 12'-0"
Stepped Clg.

Pantry

Walk-In Shower

Ln.

Wine Cellar

Dining Room
11'-8" x 13'-9"
10'-8" to 12'-0"
Stepped Clg.
Buffet

Living Room
16'-9" x 14'-0"
14'-8" to 16'-0"
Stepped Clg.

Study
13'-4" x 17'-2"
12'-0" to 13'-0"
Coffered Clg.

Master Suite
22'-8" x 16'-8"
12'-0" to 13'-4"
Tray Clg.

Wet Bar

Up

Bedroom 2
18'-3" x 12'-0"
10'-0" Clg.

Butler's Pantry

Make-Up Area

WIC

Art Niche

Morning Kitchen
18'-8" Clg.

WIC

Foyer
14'-8" Clg.

Bath 2
10'-0" Clg.

Walk-In Shower

WIC

Bedroom 1
15'-0" x 13'-6"
12'-0" Clg.

Entry
Vaulted Clg.

Master Bathroom
12'-6" to 13'-0"
Tray Clg.

Make-Up Area

Whirlpool

Bath 1
9'-4" Clg.

Walk-In Shower

Walk-In Shower

Privacy Garden

Utility
15'-10" x 6'-0"
10'-0" Clg.

Garage
22'-3" x 31'-5"
12'-0" Clg.

© THE SATER DESIGN COLLECTION, INC.

2ND FLOOR

© THE SATER DESIGN COLLECTION, INC.

Open to Below

Deck
26'-10" x 30'-2"
9'-0" Clg.

22'-4" to 23'-4"
Coffered Clg.
Open to Below

Loft
9'-0" to 10'-0"
Coffered Clg.

Bedroom 3
12'-6" x 16'-4"
9'-0" Clg.

Bedroom 4
15'-6" x 13'-6"
9'-0" Clg.

Dn.

Walk-In Shower

WIC

WIC

Wet Bar

Bath 4

Bath 3

Niche

Make-Up Area

Lin.

Walk-In Shower

Spa Tub

PHOTO ABOVE: *The outdoor kitchen and dining area are fabulous for flawless entertaining.*

6939 | Ristano

5 Bedroom	Width: 96'0"
6 Bath	Depth: 111'0"
1st Floor:	**4,186 sq ft**
2nd Floor:	**1,378 sq ft**
Living Area:	**5,564 sq ft**

Exterior Walls: 8" CBS
Foundation: Slab
Price Code: **PSE5**

PHOTOGRAPHY MAY DIFFER FROM BLUEPRINT.
NOT AVAILABLE FOR CONSTRUCTION IN LEE,
COLLIER AND CHARLOTTE COUNTIES, FLORIDA.

Martinique

PHOTOGRAPHY BY: KIM SARGENT

PHOTO ABOVE: *Clearly Mediterranean-inspired, with pavers and barrel-tile roof in terracotta hues and graceful arches and columns, the sun-drenched façade of this home extends a formal welcome. Crisp, white trim speaks of Spanish influence, and iron detailing adds a hint of non-conformity.*

PHOTO RIGHT: *Stunning wallpaper treatment and dramatic hand-painted cabinetry infuse this powder bath with eclectic elegance.*

PHOTO ABOVE: *Elegant arches and gleaming wood columns define the dining space while giving it a unique connection to the diamond-shaped living room. More wood adds drama to a stepped ceiling, and three dramatic windows provide natural light and an effortless connection to the veranda.*

PHOTO LEFT: *A stepped ceiling with molding details and elegant lighting crowns a generous master suite. An art niche separates two walk-in closets and provides a visually appealing entry to a fully appointed master bedroom.*

PHOTO ABOVE: *The hand-crafted built-in entertainment center and molded ceiling details provide drama to the large leisure room, which opens seamlessly onto the veranda's outdoor kitchen and main entertainment space.*

PHOTO RIGHT: *A chef's dream! Well-appointed and well-planned, this kitchen boasts ample storage for tools of the trade and two large islands that add lots of workspace. Ornate woodwork on the cabinetry and soffits adds an exotic flair to this ultra-functional room.*

PHOTO ABOVE: *Wood beams add rich detail to the living room's stepped ceiling, while angled walls of glass fuse this fabulous entertaining space with the veranda. Intricate molding customizes the ceiling and window edges.*

PHOTO LEFT: *This extra-large study has it all: a wall of custom cabinetry, another of windows overlooking a front garden, a stepped ceiling and lots of floor space for working and relaxing.*

PHOTO ABOVE: *The dramatic lanai features 12-foot ceilings and wraps along the entire back of the house and around the pool for first-class outdoor living and entertaining.*

PHOTO RIGHT: *A whirlpool tub in the master bath is anything but ordinary, nestled between dark wood columns and overlooking a private garden.*

PHOTO FAR RIGHT: *A carefully attended guest suite opens onto a unique garden and features a generous bath and walk-in closet.*

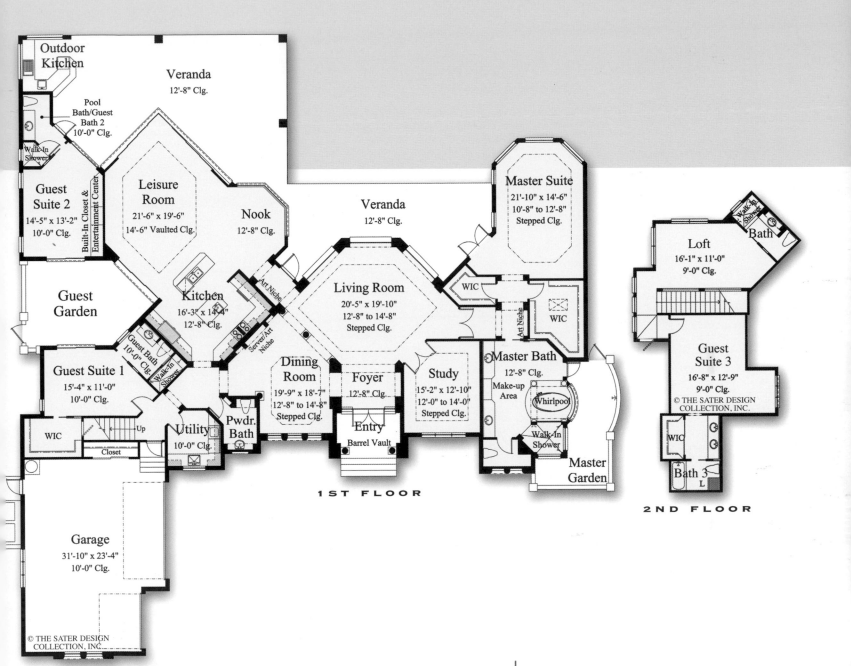

Outdoor Kitchen

Veranda
12'-8" Clg.

Pool Bath/Guest Bath 2
10'-0" Clg.

Walk-In Shower

Guest Suite 2
14'-5" x 13'-2"
10'-0" Clg.

Built-In Closet & Entertainment Center

Leisure Room
21'-6" x 19'-6"
14'-6" Vaulted Clg.

Nook
12'-8" Clg.

Veranda
12'-8" Clg.

Master Suite
21'-10" x 14'-6"
10'-8" to 12'-8"
Stepped Clg.

Guest Garden

Kitchen
16'-3" x 14'-4"
12'-8" Clg.

Art Niche

WIC

WIC

Art Niche

Living Room
20'-5" x 19'-10"
12'-8" to 14'-8"
Stepped Clg.

Guest Bath
10'-0" Clg.

Walk-In Shower

Server/Art Niche

Guest Suite 1
15'-4" x 11'-0"
10'-0" Clg.

Dining Room
19'-9" x 18'-7"
12'-8" to 14'-8"
Stepped Clg.

Foyer
12'-8" Clg.

Study
15'-2" x 12'-10"
12'-0" to 14'-0"
Stepped Clg.

Master Bath
12'-8" Clg.

Make-up Area

Whirlpool

WIC

Utility
10'-0" Clg.

Pwdr. Bath

Entry
Barrel Vault

Walk-In Shower

Master Garden

Closet

Up

Garage
31'-10" x 23'-4"
10'-0" Clg.

© THE SATER DESIGN COLLECTION, INC.

1ST FLOOR

2ND FLOOR

Loft
16'-1" x 11'-0"
9'-0" Clg.

Walk-In Shower

Bath

Guest Suite 3
16'-8" x 12'-9"
9'-0" Clg.

© THE SATER DESIGN COLLECTION, INC.

WIC

Bath 3

6932 | Martinique

5 Bedroom   Width: 94'10"

5-1/2 Bath   Depth: 103'5"

1st Floor: **3,745 sq ft**

2nd Floor: **747 sq ft**

Living Area: **4,492 sq ft**

Exterior Walls: 8" CBS

Foundation: Slab

Price Code: **PSE5**

Alamosa

PHOTOGRAPHY BY: MICHAEL LOWRY

PHOTO ABOVE: *True to its Spanish Revival heritage — low-pitched hipped roofs, an elaborate carved entry, red barrel tile and a stately cupola — this spectacular estate home is an eight-thousand-square-foot work of art. It is no surprise whatsoever that this design garnered a First Place "Parade of Homes" award.*

PHOTO RIGHT: *The very definition of a "room with a view," the Grand Solana demonstrates beautifully this layout's love affair with the great outdoors and the scenic opportunities it presents.*

PHOTO ABOVE: *The massive, ornately carved hearth of a two-sided fireplace both anchors and warms the Grand Solana and the majestic foyer. Corinthian columns support soaring volume ceilings like gods of mythology bearing the weight of the heavens.*

PHOTO LEFT: *The formal dining room, with its barrel-vault ceiling, carved coffers and mural-covered walls, displays an almost surreal beauty — the kind one sees more in a still-life painting than a photograph.*

PHOTO ABOVE: *Sequestered in a far corner of the floor plan, this opulent master suite with circular sitting room provides essential seclusion and tranquility.*

PHOTO ABOVE: *Reminiscent of the tiered arches and Tuscan columns of Rome's Colosseum, this splendid, sun-drenched Solana is nothing short of remarkable.*

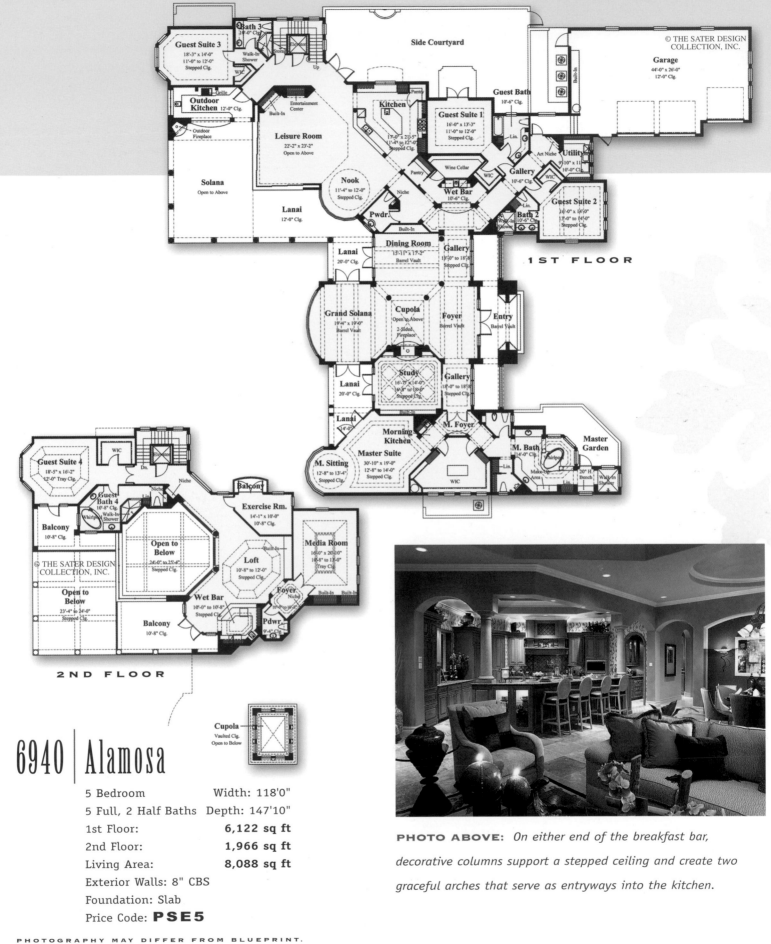

1ST FLOOR

Guest Suite 3
18'-3" x 14'-0"
11'-0" to 12'-0"
Stepped Clg.

Bath 3
14'-0" Clg.

Walk-In Shower

Up

Side Courtyard

© THE SATER DESIGN COLLECTION, INC.

Garage
44'-0" x 26'-0"
12'-0" Clg.

Built-In

Outdoor Kitchen 12'-0" Clg.

Outdoor Fireplace

Grille

Entertainment Center

Built-In

Kitchen
17'-0" x 21'-5"

Pantry

Guest Bath
10'-6" Clg.

Guest Suite 1
16'-0" x 13'-3"
11'-0" to 12'-0"
Stepped Clg.

Lin.

Art Niche

Utility
9'-10" x 11'
10'-0" Clg.

Leisure Room
22'-2" x 23'-2"
Open to Above

Solana
Open to Above

Nook
11'-4" to 12'-0"
Stepped Clg.

Lanai
12'-0" Clg.

Pantry

Wine Cellar

Niche

Wet Bar
10'-6" Clg.

WIC

Gallery
10'-6" Clg.

WIC

Guest Suite 2
16'-0" x 14'-0"
13'-0" to 14'-0"
Stepped Clg.

Pwdr.

Built-In

Bath 2
10'-6" Clg.

Walk-In Shower

Lanai
20'-0" Clg.

Dining Room
15'-11" x 17'-3"
Barrel Vault

Gallery
13'-0" to 18'-8"
Stepped Clg.

Grand Solana
19'-4" x 19'-0"
Barrel Vault

Cupola
Open to Above

Foyer
Barrel Vault

Entry
Barrel Vault

2-Sided Fireplace

Lanai
20'-0" Clg.

Study
16'-11" x 14'-0"
16'-5" to 18'-0"
Stepped Clg.

Gallery
18'-0" to 18'-8"
Stepped Clg.

Built-In

Lanai
14'-0"

Morning Kitchen

M. Foyer

M. Bath
14'-0" Clg.

Master Garden

M. Sitting
12'-8" to 13'-4"
Stepped Clg.

Master Suite
30'-10" x 19'-0"
12'-8" to 14'-0"
Stepped Clg.

WIC

Whirlpool

Lin.

Make-Up Area

20" H. Bench

Walk-In Shower

2ND FLOOR

Guest Suite 4
18'-5" x 16'-2"
12'-0" Tray Clg.

WIC

Dn.

Niche

Balcony

Guest Bath 4
10'-8" Clg.
Walk-In Shower

Whirlpool

Niche

Balcony
10'-8" Clg.

Open to Below
24'-0" x 25'-4"
Stepped Clg.

Loft
10'-8" x 12'-0"
Stepped Clg.

Built-In

Exercise Rm.
14'-1" x 10'-0"
10'-8" Clg.

Media Room
16'-0" x 20'-0"
10'-8" to 12'-0"
Tray Clg.

Built-In

© THE SATER DESIGN COLLECTION, INC.

Open to Below
23'-4" x 24'-0"
Stepped Clg.

Wet Bar
10'-0" to 10'-8"
Stepped Clg.

Balcony
10'-8" Clg.

Foyer

Niche

Pdwr.
9'-4" Clg.

Built-In

Cupola
Vaulted Clg.
Open to Below

6940 | Alamosa

5 Bedroom

5 Full, 2 Half Baths

1st Floor:	**6,122 sq ft**
2nd Floor:	**1,966 sq ft**
Living Area:	**8,088 sq ft**

Width: 118'0"

Depth: 147'10"

Exterior Walls: 8" CBS

Foundation: Slab

Price Code: **PSE5**

PHOTO ABOVE: *On either end of the breakfast bar, decorative columns support a stepped ceiling and create two graceful arches that serve as entryways into the kitchen.*

Porto Velho

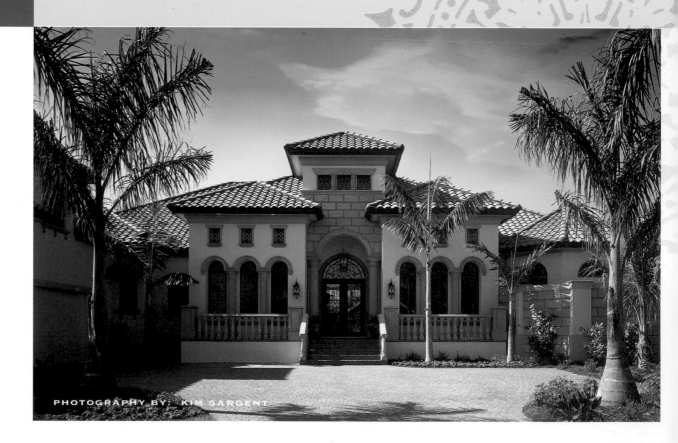

PHOTOGRAPHY BY: KIM SARGENT

PHOTO ABOVE: *Repeating arches hint of a seaside resort in this fabulous Mediterranean manor. The recessed and turreted entryway sets a welcoming invitation to the 4,500 square feet of European charm, custom details and wide-open views waiting inside.*

PHOTO RIGHT: *Scrolling ironwork turns double glass doors into works of art in this foyer, where opportunities for huge vistas are found in every direction.*

PHOTO ABOVE: The triple arches of the front façade are creatively repeated inside as pass-through points between the kitchen and great room. A vaulted, beamed ceiling and entire wall of pocketing glass add volumes of fresh-air living opportunities to this charming family space.

PHOTO LEFT: Ultra-elegant, this kitchen has custom cabinetry, a furniture-style island, and rich Tuscan details in the stove hood and tile backsplash.

PHOTO ABOVE: *Floor-to-ceiling glass panels embrace a sitting nook, and others slide open to a private end of the verandah in this luscious master suite, which also boasts a stepped ceiling, two walk-in closets and an equally stunning bathroom.*

PHOTO RIGHT: *A wood-encased, spa-style tub sits center stage in this sumptuous master bath. Behind the curved and wrought-iron-adorned wall is a walk-in shower with views to a private garden.*

PHOTO ABOVE: *Idyllic in every way, this courtyard – with its stunning stone fireplace and gazebo-style, open-beamed canopy – has an arbor-like ambience perfect for a cool drink and warm friends.*

PHOTO RIGHT: *A twilight glow highlights the indoor-outdoor connections of this home as the public and private rooms cast their personalities outside to the meandering verandah and glittering pool.*

PHOTO ABOVE: *Recessed custom cabinetry, a beamed, stepped ceiling and tall windows to the front provide elegance and light to this entrancing study located near the master bedroom.*

PHOTO RIGHT: *Just off the foyer, this dining room emanates Old World charm and details with its hand-painted ceiling, tall arched windows and intricately patterned floor.*

PHOTO FAR RIGHT: *Fine artwork and an antique console are never more at home than in this dramatic full-length niche in the master-suite foyer.*

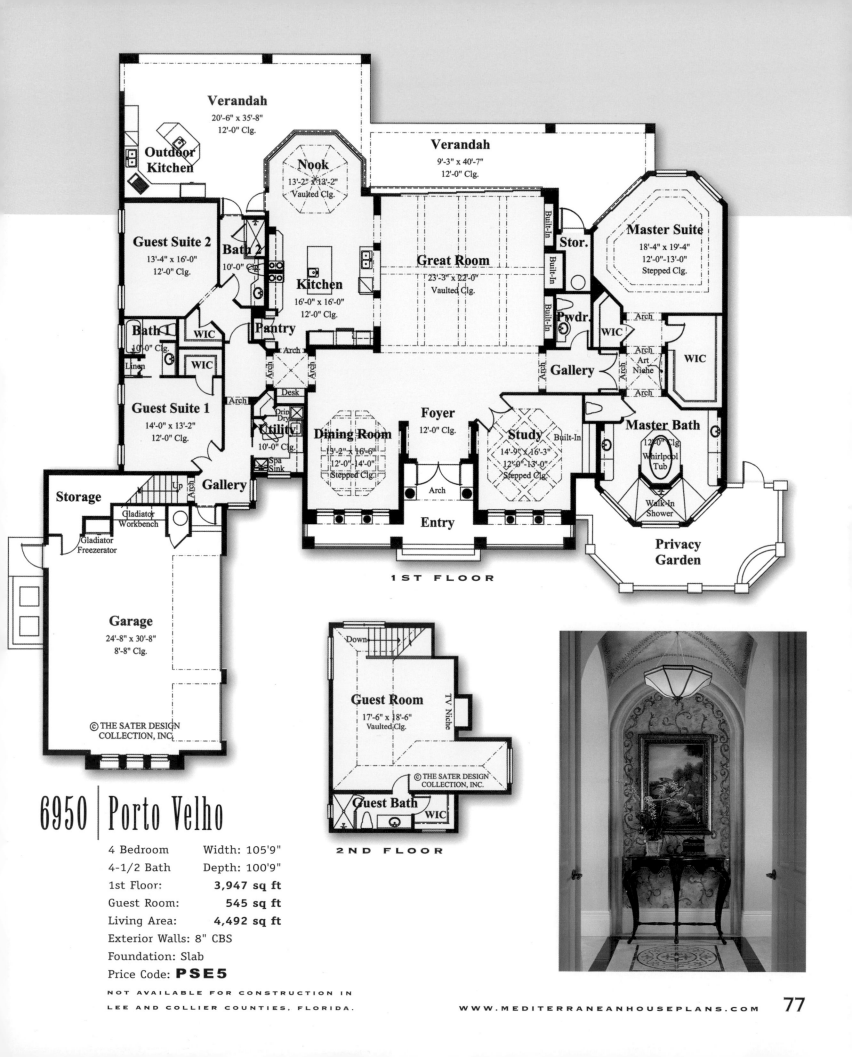

Verandah
20'-6" x 35'-8"
12'-0" Clg.

Outdoor Kitchen

Guest Suite 2
13'-4" x 16'-0"
12'-0" Clg.

Bath 2
10'-0" Clg.

Nook
13'-2" x 13'-2"
Vaulted Clg.

Verandah
9'-3" x 40'-7"
12'-0" Clg.

Stor.

Master Suite
18'-4" x 19'-4"
12'-0"-13'-0"
Stepped Clg.

Kitchen
16'-0" x 16'-0"
12'-0" Clg.

Great Room
23'-3" x 22'-0"
Vaulted Clg.

Bath 1
10'-0" Clg.

WIC

Pantry

Built-In

Built-In

Built-In

Pwdr.

WIC

Arch

Arch
Art
Niche

WIC

Linen

WIC

Arch

Arch

Arch

Arch

Arch

Gallery

Arch

Guest Suite 1
14'-0" x 13'-2"
12'-0" Clg.

Arch

Desk

Drip
Dry

Utility
10'-0" Clg.

Dining Room
13'-2" x 16'-6"
12'-0"-14'-0"
Stepped Clg.

Foyer
12'-0" Clg.

Study
14'-9" x 16'-3"
12'-0"-13'-0"
Stepped Clg.

Built-In

Master Bath
12'-0" Clg.
Whirlpool
Tub

Spa
Sink

Arch

Entry

Walk-In
Shower

Storage

Up

Gallery

Privacy Garden

Gladiator
Workbench

Gladiator
Freezerator

Arch

Garage
24'-8" x 30'-8"
8'-8" Clg.

© THE SATER DESIGN
COLLECTION, INC.

1ST FLOOR

Down

Guest Room
17'-6" x 18'-6"
Vaulted Clg.

TV Niche

© THE SATER DESIGN
COLLECTION, INC.

Guest Bath

WIC

2ND FLOOR

6950 | Porto Velho

4 Bedroom	Width: 105'9"
4-1/2 Bath	Depth: 100'9"

1st Floor:	**3,947 sq ft**
Guest Room:	**545 sq ft**
Living Area:	**4,492 sq ft**

Exterior Walls: 8" CBS

Foundation: Slab

Price Code: **PSE5**

NOT AVAILABLE FOR CONSTRUCTION IN
LEE AND COLLIER COUNTIES, FLORIDA.

WWW.MEDITERRANEANHOUSEPLANS.COM

Cataldi

PHOTOGRAPHY BY: LAURENCE TAYLOR

PHOTO ABOVE: *This majestic Mediterranean villa, rich in Renaissance and Moorish architectural heritage, basks in the late-afternoon sun under a sky as deep and blue as the Adriatic Sea.*

PHOTO RIGHT: *Adjacent to the master suite, this private study — elegantly appointed with custom built-ins and a dramatic stepped ceiling — can be either the perfect place to relax with a good book or the ideal home office.*

PHOTO FAR RIGHT: *Welcoming visitors to this stately manor home is a grand entry turret supported by stone columns.*

PHOTO ABOVE: *The great room puts family and guests in the lap of luxury. Overstuffed chairs offer ease, while a stone-arched coffer and exposed wood-beam ceiling add elegance to this restful retreat. The outdoors is welcomed through disappearing glass doors.*

PHOTO ABOVE: *A festive tile backsplash, sleek granite countertop and scenic views through the breakfast nook bay window make this gourmet kitchen the perfect place for preparing a formal meal or enjoying a casual gathering.*

PHOTO ABOVE: *The generous great room is adjacent to the kitchen and flows into the gallery, which in turn flows into the formal dining area. Volume ceilings add to the spaciousness, giving each area its own unique character.*

PHOTO LEFT: *A wraparound verandah — offering infinite entertainment opportunities — forms the boundary between a gracious indoors and an inviting backyard pool with spa.*

PHOTO ABOVE: *A prevailing cast-stone arch focuses attention to this tropical outdoor kitchen and bar. Simply add a cool drink and warm friends to complete the setting.*

PHOTO RIGHT: *One of the highlights of the generous master suite is this exquisite master bath fit for a king... and queen. Each has separate vanities and ample walk-in closets. Shared amenities include the garden whirlpool spa tub, roomy walk-in shower and scenic panorama of the home's privacy garden.*

PHOTO FAR RIGHT: *Beauty is in the details. Intricately carved organic stone materials give the master bath both boldness and intimacy, creating an environment perfect for relaxation and rejuvenation.*

Verandah
20'-6" x 35'-8"
12'-0" Clg.

Outdoor Kitchen

Arch

Arch

Verandah
9'-3" x 40'-7"
12'-0" Clg.

Nook
13'-2" x 13'-2"
12'-0" Clg.

Master Suite
18'-4" x 19'-4"
12'-0" - 13'-0"
Stepped Clg.

Storage

Built-Ins

Great Room
23'-3" x 22'-0"
Vaulted Clg.

Entertainment Center

Built-Ins

Arch

Arch

Guest Suite 2
13'-4" x 16'-0"
12'-0" Clg.

Bath 2

Pwdr

Kitchen
15'-0" x 16'-7"
12'-0" Clg.

Arch

WIC

Arch

W.I.C.
7'-9" x 12'-11"

Master Foyer

Arch

Arch

WIC

Bath 1

WIC

Linen

Master Bath
10'-0" Clg.

Make-Up Area

Built-In

Study
14'-10" x 16'-3"
12'-0" - 13'-0"
Stepped Clg.

Gallery
12'-0" Clg.

Foyer
12'-0" Clg.

Dining
13'-2" x 16'-6"
12'-0" x 14'-0"
Stepped Clg.

Desk

Arch

Utility
7'-2" x 9'-4"

Guest Suite
14'-0" x 13'-2"
12'-0" Clg.

Walk-In Shower

Arch

Up

Desk

Storage

Entry

Privacy Garden

1ST FLOOR

3-Car Garage
24'-8" x 30'-8"
8'-8" Clg.

© THE SATER DESIGN COLLECTION, INC.

Down

Entertainment Center

Guest Bedroom
17'-6" x 18'-6"
Vaulted Clg.

© THE SATER DESIGN COLLECTION, INC.

WIC

Guest Bath

2ND FLOOR

6946 | Cataldi

4 Bedroom   Width: 105'9"

4-1/2 Bath   Depth: 100'9"

1st Floor: **3,947 sq ft**

2nd Floor: **545 sq ft**

Living Area: **4,492 sq ft**

Exterior Walls: 8" CBS

Foundation: Slab

Price Code: **PSE5**

Dauphino

PHOTOGRAPHY BY: LAURENCE TAYLOR

PHOTO ABOVE: *A grand, triple-arched entrance greets you upon entering this spectacular Mediterranean-style home. Surrounded by colorful gardens and lush, tropical beauty, the design distinctively blends luxury, livability and a love of the outdoors.*

PHOTO RIGHT: *The leisure room practically floats into the veranda with three walls of sliding glass doors that fuse the space with nature.*

PHOTO FAR RIGHT: *Arch-top transom windows and doors reveal the veranda beyond. A stately fireplace radiates as a warm focal point.*

PLAN 6933

PHOTO ABOVE: *Columns connected by soft arches create a sense of flow in the grand foyer of this home. A dramatic angled staircase offers elegant ascent to a pampering second-level guest suite.*

PHOTO RIGHT: *The private study — just off the foyer and adjacent to the master suite — is comfortably outfitted with wooden floors, richly elegant built-in cabinets, and French doors to the veranda.*

PHOTO ABOVE: *Granite countertops and inlaid stone floors add refined elegance to the kitchen, while commercial-grade appliances and a menu-planning desk offer state-of-the-art amenities for the serious chef. Faux and tile walls add ambient warmth.*

PHOTO LEFT: *A generously open arrangement connects the leisure room, kitchen and morning nook, which is complemented by a bowed window and buffet server. This space is perfect for lively entertaining and family movie nights.*

PHOTO ABOVE: *Graceful arches and columns provide an elegant perimeter for a meandering veranda. An outdoor kitchen makes this an ideal venue for large-scale entertaining.*

PHOTO RIGHT: *The view from the spacious master suite is as grand as the room itself. Floor-to-ceiling windows and sliding glass doors beckon to a breezy, wraparound veranda.*

PHOTO FAR RIGHT: *A whirlpool tub, walk-in shower and tranquil garden make the master-bath a relaxing retreat at the end of a busy day.*

Outdoor Kitchen
12'-0" Clg.

Veranda
12'-0" Clg.

Leisure Room
28'-2" x 26'-3"
Pyramid Clg.

Nook
12'-0" Clg.

Powder Bath
10'-0" Clg.

Veranda
20'-4" Clg.

Veranda
12'-0" Clg.

Sitting
10'-8" 5'-2"
12'-0" Clg.

Veranda
12'-0" Clg.

Kitchen
24'-0" x 17'-1"
11'-0" to 12'-0"
Stepped Clg.

Dining Room
13'-10" x 15'-3"
16'-0" to 18'-0"
Stepped Clg.

Living Room
22'-3" x 16'-8"
20'-4" to 22'-8"
Stepped Clg.

2-Sided Fireplace

Study
18'-4" x 18'-4"
16'-0" to 17'-0"
Coffered Clg.

Master Suite
21'-8" x 14'-0"
12'-0" to 14'-0"
Stepped Clg.

Linen

Art Niche

Butler Pantry

Storage

Gallery
10'-0" Clg.

Up

WIC

Art Niche

Guest Suite 2
23'-6" x 13'-0"
10'-0" Clg.

WIC

Foyer
18'-0" to 18'-8"
Stepped Clg.

Art Niche

WIC

Make-up Area

WIC

Master Bath

Guest Bath 2

Walk-In Shower

Guest Bath 1
10'-0" Clg.

Entry
20'-4" Clg.

Walk-In Shower
12'-0" Clg.

Walk-In Shower

Guest Suite 1
15'-5" x 14'-0"
14'-0" Clg.

Utility
10'-0" Clg.

Whirlpool

Master Garden

1ST FLOOR

Garage
12'-0" Clg.

© THE SATER DESIGN COLLECTION, INC.

Balcony

© THE SATER DESIGN COLLECTION, INC.

Guest Suite
26'-7" x 15'-1"
10'-8" Clg.

Guest Bath
10'-0" Clg.

WIC

Art Niche

Storage

Walk-In Shower

Mech.

Dn

Art Niche

2ND FLOOR

6933 | Dauphino

4 Bedroom	Width: 132'8"
4-1/2 Bath	Depth: 117'3"
1st Floor:	**5,307 sq ft**
2nd Floor:	**497 sq ft**
Living Area:	**5,804 sq ft**

Exterior Walls: CBS
Foundation: Slab
Price Code: **PSE5**

Sterling Oaks

PHOTOGRAPHY BY: LAURENCE TAYLOR

PHOTO ABOVE: *Renaissance influence is evident in this Italianate-style Mediterranean villa. Decorative columns, arches and balusters give this resort home its countenance of timeless grace and beauty.*

PHOTO RIGHT: *Fluid arches – in a mirrored alcove, window and ceiling — give the formal dining area an aura of tranquility.*

PHOTO FAR RIGHT: *This stunning living room is replete with grand amenities, including a majestic stone fireplace and soaring coffered ceiling. Tuscan columns define its elegant boundaries.*

PHOTO ABOVE: *The comforts of home meet the great outdoors when the leisure room's retreating glass walls are opened to embrace a breezy verandah.*

PHOTO RIGHT: *A second-story balcony bounded by wrought-iron balustrades extends from the rear elevation, offering stellar star-gazing opportunities. Two stories of curved glass meet at the water's edge to create a stunning focal point on the verandah.*

PHOTO ABOVE: As viewed from the master suite, the rear elevation is well-lit and inviting. Around every corner, a window, archway or balcony welcomes in the outdoors.

PHOTO LEFT: The living room's curved coffered ceiling, as grand as it is, serves merely as the stage for the star performer — a spectacular, twenty-two-foot, bowed glass wall.

PHOTO ABOVE: An outdoor entertainer's paradise complete with outdoor kitchen, the verandah can easily accommodate a party of two hundred or, if you prefer, a party of two.

PHOTO RIGHT: Entertaining is once again the theme in the spacious kitchen, which boasts generous portions of everything from food-preparation and pantry space to built-in appliances and breakfast-bar seating. The ornamental hood and cabinet moldings add a Tuscan flair.

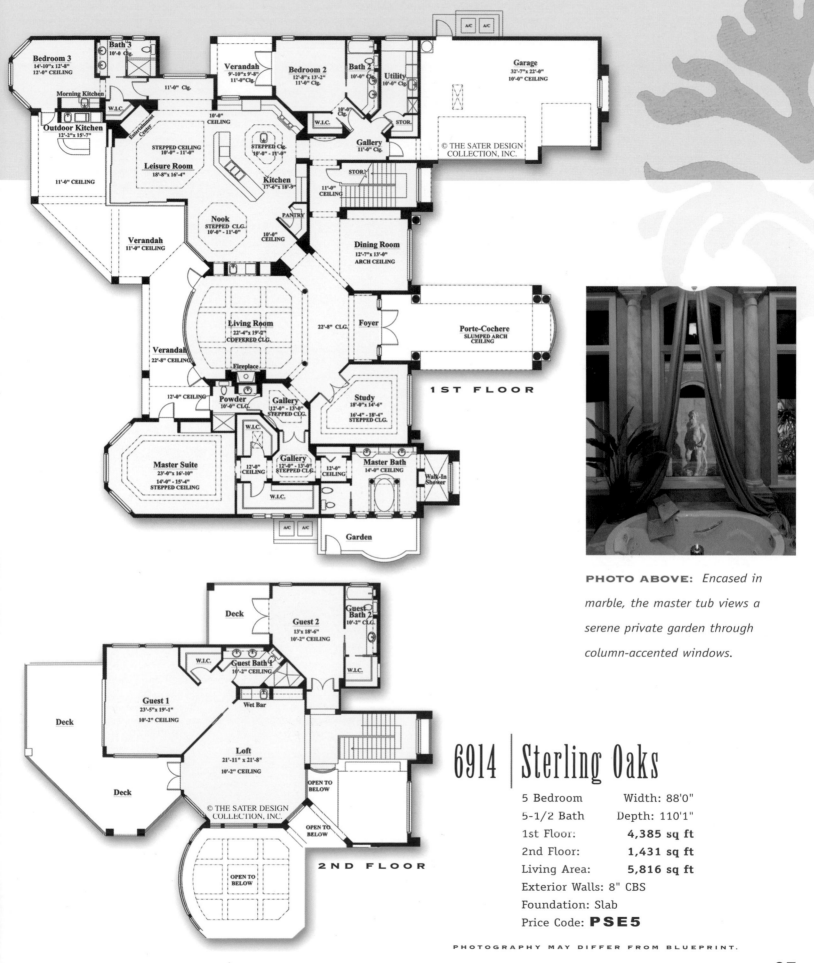

1ST FLOOR

Bedroom 3
14'-10" x 12'-8"
12'-0" CEILING

Bath 3
10'-0" Clg.

Morning Kitchen

W.I.C.

Outdoor Kitchen
12'-2" x 15'-7"

11'-0" CEILING

Verandah
11'-0" CEILING

11'-0" Clg.

Entertainment Center

Leisure Room
18'-8" x 16'-4"

STEPPED CEILING
10'-0" - 11'-0"

10'-0" CEILING

Verandah
9'-10" x 9'-8"
11'-0" Clg.

Bedroom 2
12'-8" x 13'-2"
11'-0" Clg.

Bath 2
10'-0" Clg.

Utility
10'-0" Clg.

Garage
32'-7" x 22'-0"
10'-0" CEILING

A/C A/C

STEPPED Clg.
10'-0" - 11'-0"

W.I.C.

STOR.

Gallery
11'-0" Clg.

© THE SATER DESIGN COLLECTION, INC.

Kitchen
17'-6" x 18'-9"

Nook
STEPPED CLG.
10'-0" - 11'-0"

PANTRY

10'-0" CEILING

STOR.

11'-0" CEILING

Dining Room
12'-7" x 13'-0"
ARCH CEILING

Living Room
22'-4" x 19'-2"
COFFERED CLG.

22'-8" CLG.

Foyer

Porte-Cochere
SLUMPED ARCH CEILING

Verandah
22'-8" CEILING

Fireplace

12'-0" CEILING

Powder
10'-0" CLG.

Gallery
12'-0" - 13'-0"
STEPPED CLG.

Study
18'-0" x 14'-6"
16'-4" - 18'-4"
STEPPED CLG.

W.I.C.

Gallery
12'-0" - 13'-0"
STEPPED CLG.

Master Suite
23'-0" x 16'-10"
14'-0" - 15'-4"
STEPPED CEILING

12'-0" CEILING

12'-0" CEILING

Master Bath
14'-0" CEILING

Walk-In Shower

W.I.C.

A/C A/C

Garden

PHOTO ABOVE: *Encased in marble, the master tub views a serene private garden through column-accented windows.*

2ND FLOOR

Deck

Guest 2
13' x 18'-6"
10'-2" CEILING

Guest Bath 2
10'-2" Clg.

W.I.C.

Guest Bath 1
10'-2" CEILING

W.I.C.

Guest 1
23'-5" x 19'-1"
10'-2" CEILING

Deck

Deck

Wet Bar

Loft
21'-11" x 21'-8"
10'-2" CEILING

OPEN TO BELOW

OPEN TO BELOW

OPEN TO BELOW

© THE SATER DESIGN COLLECTION, INC.

6914 | Sterling Oaks

5 Bedroom	Width: 88'0"
5-1/2 Bath	Depth: 110'1"
1st Floor:	**4,385 sq ft**
2nd Floor:	**1,431 sq ft**
Living Area:	**5,816 sq ft**

Exterior Walls: 8" CBS

Foundation: Slab

Price Code: **PSE5**

Saraceno

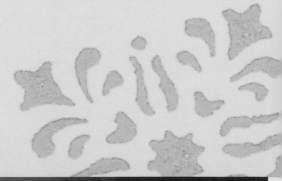

PHOTOGRAPHY BY: LAURENCE TAYLOR

PHOTO ABOVE: *Arches and simple lines dominate the classic Mediterranean architecture of this home, while corbels, banding, and hipped and pavilion roofs provide visual excitement. A wide, curving driveway leads graciously to a side-entry garage, and the cozy front porch welcomes guests with classic railings and double doors leading to a stately foyer.*

PHOTO RIGHT: *A unique shower floats effortlessly in a sea of glass, with soothing views to the privacy garden that are shared by the elegant, marble-encased bathtub. At the other end of the room are two substantial walk-in closets. The granite-topped vanity has a makeup nook and dramatic lighting.*

PHOTO FAR RIGHT: *Natural light streams into the leisure room through zero-corner sliding glass doors and a second-story band of vertical windows, opening up this room to the outdoors.*

PHOTO ABOVE: *Just steps from the wet bar, living room and kitchen, the dining room is the focal point for formal dinners and special-occasion Sunday brunches.*

PHOTO RIGHT: *An abundance of glass — in windows, nooks and disappearing walls to major living spaces — allows this home to celebrate the outdoors. The meandering veranda includes an outdoor kitchen perfect for family celebrations.*

PHOTO ABOVE: *Dignity characterizes the master suite, where two tray ceilings, dramatic windows and a sliding wall adjacent to the veranda define the room as a worthy retreat.*

Veranda

Outdoor Kitchen

Leisure
13'-5" x 13'-4"
22'-0" Clg.

Nook
13'-7" x 7'-9"
9'-8" - 10'-0" Clg.

Niche

Sitting

Veranda

Master Suite
29'-0" x 21'-4"
11'-0" - 13'-0" Clg.

Bedroom 3
14'-6" x 14'-0"
10'-0" Clg.

Kitchen
16'-3" x 15'-4"
9'-4" - 10'-0" Clg.

Pool Bath

W.I.C.

Bath 3

Niche

Pantry

Bar

Living
22'-0" x 28'-0"
12'-0" - 14'-0" Clg.

Fireplace

Niche

Morning Kitchen

W.I.C.

Bedroom 2
15'-2" x 11'-5"
10'-0" Clg.

Bath 2

W.I.C.

Gallery

Dining
11'-0" x 13'-9"
12'-0" - 14'-0" Clg.

Niche

Foyer

W.I.C.

Study
16'-10" x 12'-0"
14'-0" - 15'-4" Clg.

Desk

Utility
11'-5" x 9'-0"
10'-0" Clg.

Entry

1ST FLOOR

Master Bath

3 Car Garage
31'-2" x 23'-0"
10'-0" Clg.

Privacy Garden

© THE SATER DESIGN COLLECTION, INC.

© THE SATER DESIGN COLLECTION, INC.

Balcony

Open to Below

Loft
16'-10" - 10'-4"
10'-4" Clg.

Bedroom 4
14'-8" x 15'-10"
9'-4" Clg.

Entertainment Center

Bath 4

W.I.C.

Mech.

2ND FLOOR

6929 | Saraceno

4 Bedroom	Width: 81'10"
5 Bath	Depth: 113'0"
1st Floor:	**4,137 sq ft**
2nd Floor:	**876 sq ft**
Living Area:	**5,013 sq ft**

Exterior Walls: 8" CBS

Foundation: Slab

Price Code: **PSE5**

Gambier Court

PHOTOGRAPHY BY: GIOVANNI PHOTOGRAPHY

PHOTO ABOVE: *The front-entry turret —
with its wrought-iron-filled friezes and recessed
glass doors – makes an impressive
Mediterranean statement.*

PHOTO RIGHT: *An absolutely extraordinary
fireplace, dramatic pergolas of carved Tuscan
columns and wood canopies, and a warm brick
floor all merge to create a courtyard worthy
of royalty.*

PHOTO ABOVE: Lavish get-togethers, as well as cozy family nights, are memory-makers in this leisure room with its coffered ceiling, rich stone floor, striking entertainment niche and disappearing glass walls to the courtyard.

PHOTO LEFT: Gleaming granite countertops and a Tuscan-flavored tile backsplash are luxurious appointments to a kitchen that's also ultra-functional with its extended serving counter and center prep-island.

PLAN | 6948

PHOTO ABOVE: *A veranda wrapping the rear of the home creates a beautiful brick border around a spectacular pool, which features planters bearing lush vegetation as well as fountains. An outdoor kitchen off the leisure room is perfect for summertime parties.*

PHOTO RIGHT: *It's hard to tell where the bedroom ends and the great outdoors begins in this large and light-flooded master retreat. The sitting area is perfect for a good book – and even an afternoon nap.*

PHOTO FAR RIGHT: *A center garden tub and walk-in shower behind a marble wall make an impressive statement in this ultra luxurious master bath, which also features "his" and "hers" vanities and arch-top transom windows.*

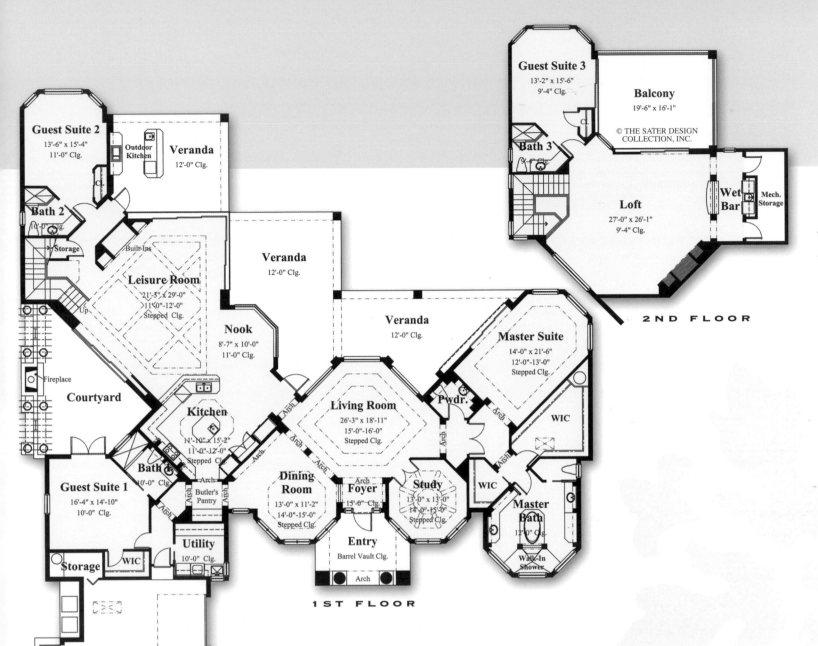

Guest Suite 3
13'-2" x 15'-6"
9'-4" Clg.

Balcony
19'-6" x 16'-1"

© THE SATER DESIGN
COLLECTION, INC.

Bath 3

Loft
27'-0" x 26'-1"
9'-4" Clg.

Wet Bar

Mech. Storage

2ND FLOOR

Guest Suite 2
13'-6" x 15'-4"
11'-0" Clg.

Outdoor Kitchen

Veranda
12'-0" Clg.

Bath 2

Storage

Built-Ins

Leisure Room
21'-3" x 29'-0"
11'-0"-12'-0"
Stepped Clg.

Veranda
12'-0" Clg.

Nook
8'-7" x 10'-0"
11'-0" Clg.

Veranda
12'-0" Clg.

Master Suite
14'-0" x 21'-6"
12'-0"-13'-0"
Stepped Clg.

Up

Fireplace

Courtyard

Kitchen
11'-10" x 15'-2"
11'-0"-12'-0"
Stepped Clg.

Living Room
26'-3" x 18'-11"
15'-0"-16'-0"
Stepped Clg.

Pwdr.

WIC

Guest Suite 1
16'-4" x 14'-10"
10'-0" Clg.

Bath

Butler's Pantry

Dining Room
13'-0" x 11'-2"
14'-0"-15'-0"
Stepped Clg.

Foyer
15'-6" Clg.

Study
13'-0" x 13'-0"
14'-0"-15'-0"
Stepped Clg.

WIC

Master Bath
12'-0" Clg.

Utility
10'-0" Clg.

Storage

WIC

Entry
Barrel Vault Clg.

Walk-In Shower

1ST FLOOR

3-Car Garage
21'-0" x 32'-10"
10'-0" Clg.

© THE SATER DESIGN
COLLECTION, INC.

6948 | Gambier Court

4 Bedroom	Width: 93'10"
4-1/2 Baths	Depth: 113'8"
1st Floor:	**3,758 sq ft**
2nd Floor:	**1,193 sq ft**
Living Area:	**4,951 sq ft**

Exterior Walls: 8" CBS
Foundation: Slab
Price Code: **PSE5**

PHOTOGRAPHY MAY DIFFER FROM BLUEPRINT.
NOT AVAILABLE FOR CONSTRUCTION IN
LEE OR COLLIER COUNTIES, FLORIDA.

Cantadora

PHOTOGRAPHY BY: CJ WALKER

PHOTO ABOVE: *A strikingly handsome entry turret, dramatically defines the façade of this palatial Mediterranean resort home and proclaims the casual elegance characteristic of New Mediterranean design.*

PHOTO RIGHT: *A soaring stepped ceiling, custom built-ins and a trio of arch-top windows make a restful retreat of this unique, octagonal-shaped study adjacent to the master suite.*

PHOTO ABOVE: *This view of the living room from the formal dining area speaks volumes about the design's blending of interior and exterior spaces. A sixteen-foot stepped ceiling and expansive glass create a seamless boundary between indoors and out.*

PHOTO LEFT: *Casual and comfortable, yet equipped to meet any culinary challenge, the kitchen flows into both the leisure room and the breakfast nook. The gleaming, carved-wood hood provides a beautiful focal point.*

PHOTO ABOVE: *Architectural lighting gives the rear elevation a warm glow in the early evening hours. With its outdoor kitchen and ample entertainment areas, the veranda is perfect for an intimate gathering of two or a get-together of twenty.*

PHOTO RIGHT: *The leisure room has it all, from custom built-ins for media equipment to an outdoor kitchen located just beyond zero-corner sliding glass doors.*

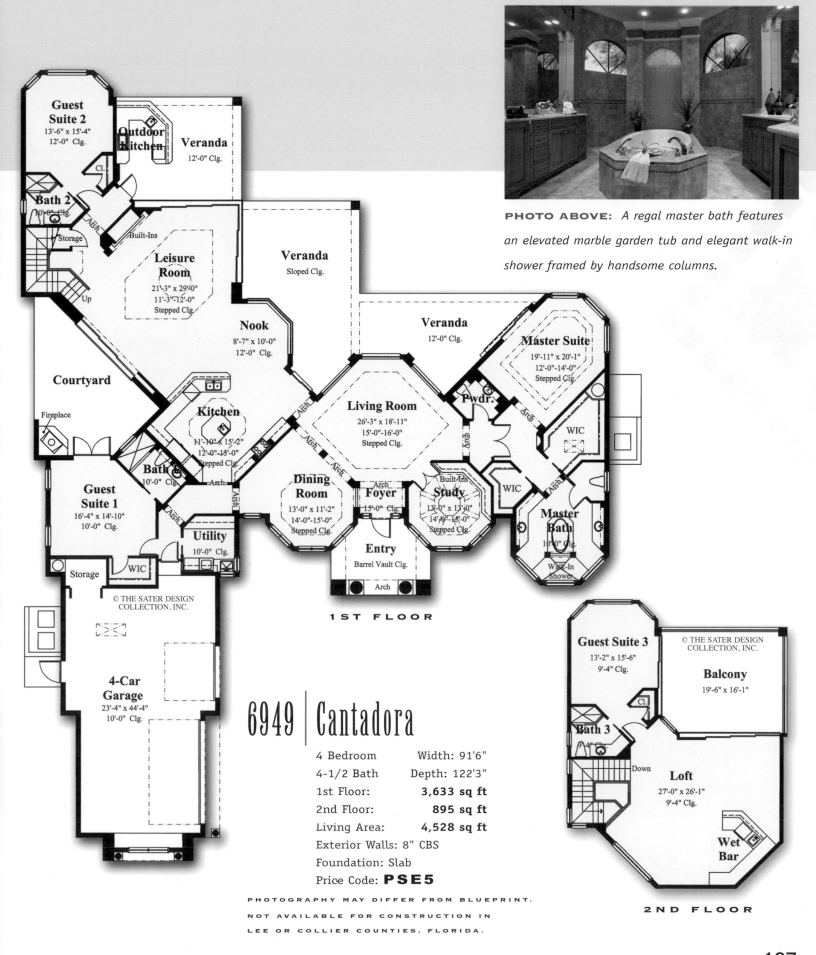

Guest Suite 2
13'-6" x 15'-4"
12'-0" Clg.

Outdoor Kitchen

Veranda
12'-0" Clg.

Cl.

Bath 2
10'-0" Clg.

Storage

Built-Ins

Leisure Room
21'-3" x 29'40"
11'-3"-12'-0"
Stepped Clg.

Up

Veranda
Sloped Clg.

Veranda
12'-0" Clg.

Master Suite
19'-11" x 20'-1"
12'-0"-14'-0"
Stepped Clg.

Nook
8'-7" x 10'-0"
12'-0" Clg.

Courtyard

Fireplace

Kitchen
11'-10" x 15'-2"
12'-0"-13'-0"
Stepped Clg.

Living Room
26'-3" x 18'-11"
15'-0"-16'-0"
Stepped Clg.

Pwdr.

WIC

Arch

Bath
10'-0" Clg.

Guest Suite 1
16'-4" x 14'-10"
10'-0" Clg.

Dining Room
13'-0" x 11'-2"
14'-0"-15'-0"
Stepped Clg.

Arch

Foyer
15'-0" Clg.

Study
13'-0" x 13'-0"
14'-0"-15'-0"
Stepped Clg.

Built-Ins

WIC

WIC

Master Bath
10'-0" Clg.

Walk-In Shower

Utility
10'-0" Clg.

Entry
Barrel Vault Clg.

Arch

© THE SATER DESIGN COLLECTION, INC.

Storage

WIC

1ST FLOOR

4-Car Garage
23'-4" x 44'-4"
10'-0" Clg.

PHOTO ABOVE: *A regal master bath features an elevated marble garden tub and elegant walk-in shower framed by handsome columns.*

6949 | Cantadora

4 Bedroom   Width: 91'6"
4-1/2 Bath   Depth: 122'3"
1st Floor: **3,633 sq ft**
2nd Floor: **895 sq ft**
Living Area: **4,528 sq ft**
Exterior Walls: 8" CBS
Foundation: Slab
Price Code: **PSE5**

PHOTOGRAPHY MAY DIFFER FROM BLUEPRINT.

NOT AVAILABLE FOR CONSTRUCTION IN

LEE OR COLLIER COUNTIES, FLORIDA.

Guest Suite 3
13'-2" x 15'-6"
9'-4" Clg.

© THE SATER DESIGN COLLECTION, INC.

Balcony
19'-6" x 16'-1"

Cl.

Bath 3

Down

Loft
27'-0" x 26'-1"
9'-4" Clg.

Wet Bar

2ND FLOOR

Autumn Woods

PHOTOGRAPHY BY: LAURENCE TAYLOR

PHOTO ABOVE: *Winner of a first-place award from the American Institute of Building Design, this Mediterranean manor glitters like a precious gem. Guests are welcomed through a glass-paneled door sheltered by a bold entry turret.*

PHOTO RIGHT: *Tucked in a cozy section of the lanai, a Mediterranean-style fireplace brings warmth — while a dining area fountain adds ambient sound. Together they create an intimate, relaxing evening.*

PHOTO ABOVE: *A bay window offers dinner guests a panoramic view, while decorative columns stand close by, setting the boundaries between foyer and dining area.*

PHOTO LEFT: *The diamond-shaped leisure room is conveniently located adjacent to the kitchen, which mean snacks are just a few steps away. The paneled, vaulted ceiling casts a warm glow over this comfortable and relaxing space.*

PLAN | **6753**

PHOTO ABOVE: *Casual and cozy, this corner-pocket living room offers visitors a warm welcome, courtesy of its beautifully crafted tile fireplace and angled view.*

PHOTO RIGHT: *In Tuscan tradition, the kitchen is both friendly and intimate, making it as much a place for casual conversation as for cooking.*

PHOTO FAR RIGHT: *Ochre-colored stucco, terracotta tile, turquoise pool and azure sky work in concert — creating an image that one might see on a postcard from an Aegean Sea resort.*

Lanai
10'-0" Clg.

Outdoor Kitchen

Storage

Entertainment Center

Leisure Room
17'-0" x 20'-10"
Vaulted Clg.

Master Sitting

Lanai
12'-0" Clg.

Nook
11'-8" x 11'-1"
12'-0" Clg.

Fireplace

Master Suite
24'-0" x 17'-11"
13'-4" Clg.

Walk-In Shower

Kitchen
16'-9" x 18'-8"
10'-0" Clg.

W.I.C.

Personal Valet

His Bath
10'-0" Clg.

Art Niche

Living Room
22'-9" x 17'-8"
14'-0" Clg.

Powder
10'-0" Clg.

Butler's Pantry

Pantry

Her Bath
12'-0" Clg.

W.I.C.

Fireplace

W.I.C.

Bath #1
10'-0" Clg.

Whirlpool

Linen

Study
16'-11" x 20'-0"
Tongue & Groove Clg.

Foyer
Groin Vault Clg.

Dining Room
17'-6" x 18'-5"
14'-0" Clg.

Art Niche

Guest Suite #1
14'-1" x 15'-4"
10'-0" Clg.

Walk-In Shower

Utility
Iron Station

Duct W/D

Master Garden

Entry

Gallery

Guest Suite #2
12'-6" x 17'-2"
10'-0" Clg.

Bath #2
10'-0" Clg.

Built In

Walk-In Shower

Garage
23'-8" x 36'-1"
11'-0" Clg.

6753 | Autumn Woods

3 Bedroom   Width: 87'2"

4-1/2 Bath   Depth: 127'11"

Living Area: **4,534 sq ft**

Exterior Walls: 8" CBS

Foundation: Slab

Price Code: **PSE5**

PHOTOGRAPHY MAY DIFFER FROM BLUEPRINT.

Kinsey

PHOTOGRAPHY BY: CJ WALKER

PHOTO ABOVE: *A Romanesque colonnade portico sets the tone for this graciously elegant façade. Columns of the Tuscan order, arch-top windows and decorative corbels create an inviting exterior.*

PHOTO RIGHT: *A deep coffer, crown molding and an elegant stepped ceiling infuse the dining room with an air of finesse.*

PHOTO FAR RIGHT: *The formal living room overreaches its borders with disappearing walls of glass that create a stunning view of the outdoors.*

PLAN | 6756

PHOTO ABOVE: *Those who love the outdoors need never come in, given the expansiveness of this rambling covered lanai in the rear elevation.*

PHOTO RIGHT: *The gourmet kitchen is a study in symmetry. A perfect balance is struck between form and function: double ovens to one side of the stove, generously proportioned refrigerator to the other. In between? A handy center island, as well as seating for four at the angled breakfast bar.*

PHOTO FAR RIGHT: *Bathed in morning sunlight, the nook provides a perfect place to start the day.*

entertainment center
built ins

leisure
17'-0" x 19'-0"
10'-0" clg.

covered lanai
38'-0" x 10'-0"

butt joint glass

nook
9'-0" x 10'-0"
10'-0" clg.

eating bar

dry bar

master
17'-0" x 14'-8"
step clg.

server niche

pool bath

kitchen

14' x 14'

living
14'-0" x 14'-0"
step clg.

books

arch

arch

gallery

pantry

walk in wardrobe

arch

art display

arch

arch

br. 2
13'-6" x 10'-10"
10'-0" clg.

dressing

arch

books

arch

mirror

books

arch

dining
11'-6" x 15'-0"
step clg.

storage

his

study
10'-0" x 14'-0"
step clg.

foyer

arch

master bath

hers

br. 3
13'-6" x 10'-10"
10'-0" clg.

utility

privacy wall

private garden

covered entry

workbench

garage
22'-0" x 23'-8"

© THE SATER DESIGN COLLECTION, INC.

6756 | Kinsey

3 Bedroom   Width: 65'0"

2-1/2 Bath   Depth: 84'0"

Living Area: **2,907 sq ft**

Exterior Walls: 2x6 or 8" CBS

Foundation: Slab

Price Code: **C3**

PHOTOGRAPHY MAY DIFFER FROM BLUEPRINT.

Grimaldi Court

PHOTOGRAPHY BY: CJ WALKER

PHOTO ABOVE: *Celebrate the graceful arches, tapered decorative columns, carved balusters and arch-top windows that stretch to the sky. Together they foretell of the elegance and beauty waiting within this majestic Mediterranean resort home.*

PHOTO RIGHT: *A wall of curved glass is all that separates the living room from a wraparound verandah, presenting visitors with a glorious first impression as they enter the foyer.*

PHOTO ABOVE: *Earth tones — as well as a charming two-sided fireplace — warm the living and dining area. A line of decorative columns creates a majestic boundary between the foyer entry and living areas.*

PHOTO LEFT: *The wraparound verandah sparkles at sunset, the surface of a tranquil pool adding some sparkle of its own.*

PHOTO ABOVE: *The early morning sun shines through the bay window of the breakfast nook, giving it a golden glow and making it one of the most warm and welcoming spaces in the home.*

PHOTO RIGHT: *Arched entryways lead to the beautiful and functional gourmet kitchen, which boasts black granite countertops, carved-wood cabinets, a stainless-steel double oven and built-in refrigerator.*

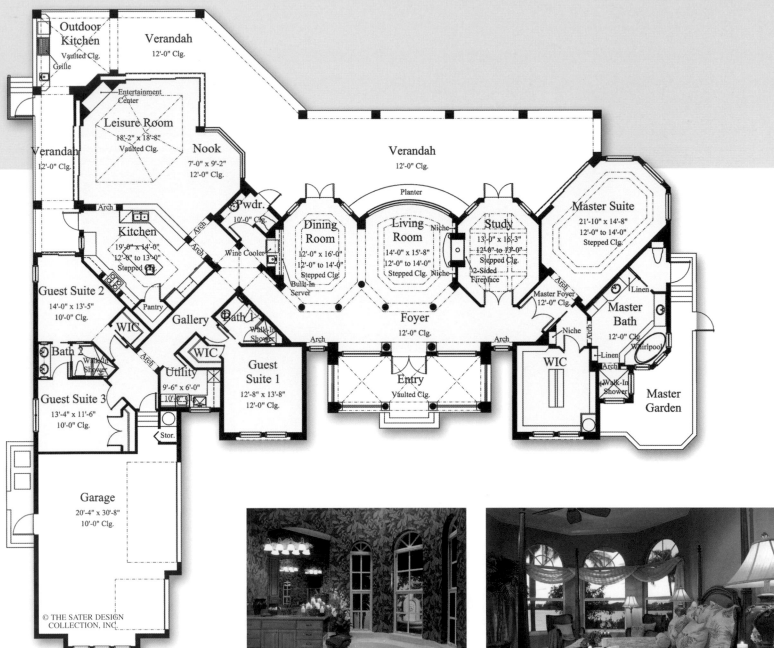

Outdoor Kitchen
Vaulted Clg.
Grille

Verandah
12'-0" Clg.

Entertainment Center

Leisure Room
18'-2" x 18'-8"
Vaulted Clg.

Nook
7'-0" x 9'-2"
12'-0" Clg.

Verandah
12'-0" Clg.

Arch

Pwdr.
10'-0" Clg.

Verandah
12'-0" Clg.

Planter

Master Suite
21'-10" x 14'-8"
12'-0" to 14'-0"
Stepped Clg.

Kitchen
19'-0" x 14'-0"
12'-8" to 13'-0"
Stepped Clg.

Arch

Wine Cooler

Dining Room
12'-0" x 16'-0"
12'-0" to 14'-0"
Stepped Clg.

Living Room
14'-0" x 15'-8"
12'-0" to 14'-0"
Stepped Clg.

Niche

Study
13'-0" x 16'-3"
12'-0" to 13'-0"
Stepped Clg.

Niche

2-Sided Fireplace

Built-In Server

Master Foyer
12'-0" Clg.

Master Bath
12'-0" Clg.
Whirlpool

Linen

Guest Suite 2
14'-0" x 13'-5"
10'-0" Clg.

WIC

Pantry

Gallery

Bath 1

Walk-In Shower

Foyer
12'-0" Clg.

Arch

Arch

Niche

Arch

Bath 2
Walk-In Shower

WIC

Utility
9'-6" x 6'-0"
10'-0"

Guest Suite 1
12'-8" x 13'-8"
12'-0" Clg.

Entry
Vaulted Clg.

WIC

Walk-In Shower

Linen
Arch

Guest Suite 3
13'-4" x 11'-6"
10'-0" Clg.

Stor.

Master Garden

Garage
20'-4" x 30'-8"
10'-0" Clg.

© THE SATER DESIGN COLLECTION, INC.

PHOTO ABOVE: *With its scenic view of the master garden, the master bath becomes a private oasis.*

PHOTO ABOVE: *Arch-top windows and retreating glass doors invite the exterior landscape into the master bedroom, transforming the outdoors into an ever-changing work of art for this elegant retreat.*

6783 | Grimaldi Court

4 Bedroom   Width: 102'4"
3-1/2 Bath   Depth: 102'4"
Living Area: **3,817 sq ft**
Exterior Walls: 8" CBS
Foundation: Slab
Price Code: **PSE5**

PHOTOGRAPHY MAY DIFFER FROM BLUEPRINT.
NOT AVAILABLE FOR CONSTRUCTION IN
LEE OR COLLIER COUNTIES, FLORIDA.

Toscana

PHOTOGRAPHY BY: TOM HARPER

PHOTO ABOVE: *Resplendent at twilight, this classic Mediterranean resort home captures the essence of its architectural heritage. Its grand façade — with characteristic turrets and majestic open entry — gives way to an interior that is spacious, casual and ideal for entertaining.*

PHOTO RIGHT: *A graceful arch creates an inviting transition into the dining room, where a pair of arch-top windows offers sunset views.*

PHOTO ABOVE: *A delightful tile-front fireplace with coffered mantle serves as an art niche, the centerpiece of an airy great room made even more spacious by retreating glass doors to the rear loggia.*

PHOTO LEFT: *Sleek in its simplicity, this contemporary gourmet kitchen boasts ample countertops, custom cabinets and state-of-the-art appliances.*

PHOTO ABOVE: *Stone columns, like stoic sentinels watching over the home's expansive loggia and pool, bring a Renaissance strength and harmony to the rear elevation. Multiple retreating glass doors erase the boundaries between interior and exterior spaces.*

PHOTO RIGHT: *A striking tray ceiling creates a sheltering canopy in this generous and gracious master suite, while retreating glass doors offer convenient access to the breezy wraparound loggia.*

PHOTO RIGHT: *"His" and "hers" vanities bookend the garden tub and walk-in shower in the octagonal-shaped master bath, a place of rest and respite at the end of a hectic day.*

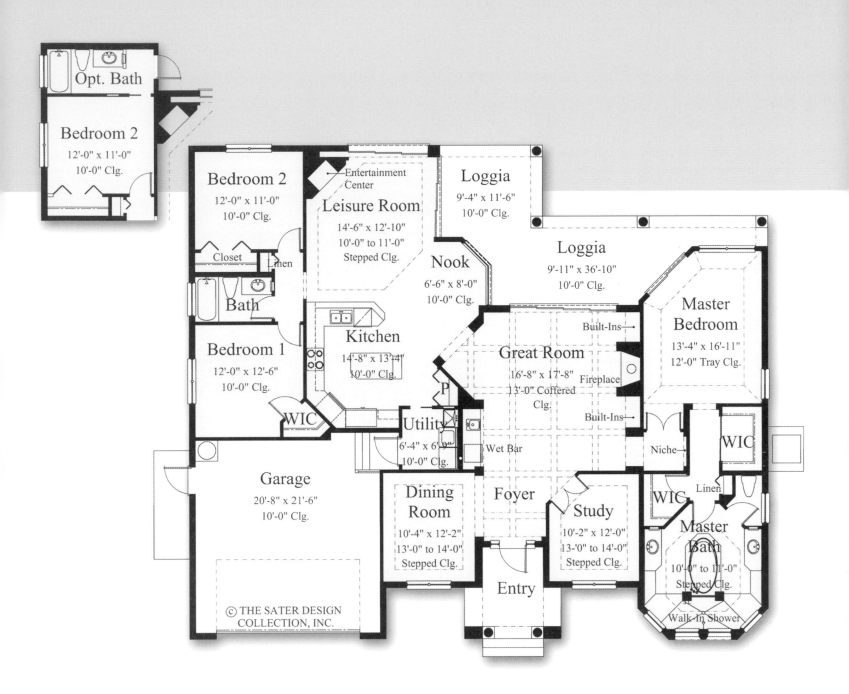

Opt. Bath

Bedroom 2
12'-0" x 11'-0"
10'-0" Clg.

Bedroom 2
12'-0" x 11'-0"
10'-0" Clg.

Entertainment Center

Leisure Room
14'-6" x 12'-10"
10'-0" to 11'-0"
Stepped Clg.

Loggia
9'-4" x 11'-6"
10'-0" Clg.

Loggia
9'-11" x 36'-10"
10'-0" Clg.

Closet

Linen

Nook
6'-6" x 8'-0"
10'-0" Clg.

Master Bedroom
13'-4" x 16'-11"
12'-0" Tray Clg.

Bath

Kitchen
14'-8" x 13'-4"
10'-0" Clg.

Built-Ins

Great Room
16'-8" x 17'-8"
13'-0" Coffered Clg.

Fireplace

Built-Ins

Bedroom 1
12'-0" x 12'-6"
10'-0" Clg.

P

WIC

Utility
6'-4" x 6'-9"
10'-0" Clg.

Wet Bar

Niche

WIC

WIC

Linen

Garage
20'-8" x 21'-6"
10'-0" Clg.

Dining Room
10'-4" x 12'-2"
13'-0" to 14'-0"
Stepped Clg.

Foyer

Study
10'-2" x 12'-0"
13'-0" to 14'-0"
Stepped Clg.

Master Bath
10'-0" to 11'-0"
Stepped Clg.

© THE SATER DESIGN COLLECTION, INC.

Entry

Walk In Shower

6758 | Toscana

3 Bedroom   Width: 65'0"
2 Bath   Depth: 55'2"
Living Area: **2,329 sq ft**
Optional Bath: **70 sq ft**
Exterior Walls: 8" CBS
Foundation: Slab
Price Code: **C2**

Monterrey Lane

PHOTOGRAPHY BY: LAURENCE TAYLOR

PHOTO ABOVE: *Modern sensibility meets Spanish Colonial heritage in this quintessential Mediterranean seaside resort home. In contrast to its casual façade, with its stucco walls and rambling, red-barrel-tile roof, the home's interior exhibits the noble simplicity and calm grandeur of classic architecture.*

PHOTO RIGHT: *Tuscan stone columns flank an intricately tiled recessed entry.*

PHOTO FAR RIGHT: *Spatial qualities of Old World architecture — the domed and vaulted spaces of ancient Rome in particular — give the formal dining area an almost cathedral-like quality.*

PLAN | 6672

PHOTO ABOVE: *In the leisure room, built-ins segue seamlessly to retreating glass doors, all under an octagonal vaulted ceiling.*

PHOTO RIGHT: *This casual, yet highly efficient gourmet kitchen gives the chef ready access to up-to-date conveniences and a large walk-in pantry.*

PHOTO TOP FAR RIGHT: *This spacious and very private master bath boasts a high stepped ceiling, garden tub, "his" and "hers" vanities and walk-in closets, making it a luxurious space fit for a king and queen.*

PHOTO BOTTOM FAR RIGHT: *The generously sized master suite affords both a sitting area and a magnificent panoramic view.*

Sitting Area

Master Suite
18'-10" x 19'-11"
11'-0" to 13'-0"
Stepped Clg.
— bed art niche

WH

Optional Valet Her WIC

Walk-in Shower

Pool Room

Lanai

Nook
12'-0" Clg.

Leisure Room
21'-4" x 19'-3"
Vaulted Clg.

Entertainment Center

Built-ins

Arch

Arch

M. Bath
13'-4" x 13'-9"
12'-0" Stepped Clg.

Niche

Arch

Niche

Arch

His WIC

Living Room
17'-0" x 23'-2"
12'-0" to 14'-0"
Stepped Ceiling

Fireplace

Arch

Arch

Arch

Wet Bar

Built-in

Kitchen
17'-0" x 16'-3"
10' Clg.

Pantry

Built-ins

WIC

Bath 2

Linen

Walk-in Shower

Study
14'-5" x 14'-9"
12'-0" to 14'-0"
Stepped Clg.

Built-in

Arch

Foyer
16'-8" Clg.

Niche   Niche

Arch

Dining
14'-0" x 14'-6"
13'-0" to 14'-0"
Stepped Clg.

Arch

Arch

Gallery

Guest Suite 2
13'-3" x 14'-6"
10'-0" Clg.

Guest Suite 1
11'-8" x 15'-0"
10'-0" Clg.

WIC

Bath 1

Iron Station

Sink Spa

Studio
Duet W/D
DryAire

WH

Outdoor Kitchen

2 Car Garage
23'-0" x 26'-10"
11'-0" Clg.

Golf Cart

AC

AC

6672 | Monterrey Lane

3 Bedroom   Width: 79'0"

4 Bath   Depth: 117'2"

Living Area: **4,009 sq ft**

Exterior Walls: 8" CBS

Foundation: Slab

Price Code: **PSE5**

PHOTOGRAPHY MAY DIFFER FROM BLUEPRINT.

Deauville

PHOTOGRAPHY BY: CJ WALKER

PHOTO ABOVE: *The noble families of Rome, like city-dwellers today, understood the need for a "countryside" home — a place where they could commune with nature in an informal setting and rejuvenate their spirits. This Italianate villa home is a classic example. As evidenced in the architectural elements of the home's façade, the Romans may have embraced country life, but the luxuries of city life were always within easy reach.*

PHOTO RIGHT: *Like a Renaissance work of art, this formal dining room gives guests a taste of true elegance. French doors open to the portico for refreshing suppers.*

PHOTO ABOVE: *Large expanses of glass create a breathtaking façade along the rambling loggia, which is supported by stately Tuscan columns.*

PHOTO LEFT: *State-of-the-art appliances make an understated appearance in the gourmet kitchen, inconspicuously supporting the chef in his or her culinary endeavors. Notice the arched niche, which makes a cozy, Tuscan-feel home for a commercial-grade range.*

PHOTO ABOVE: *Gracefully arched built-ins, like beautiful bookends, complement a carved art niche over the mantel of this charming living-room fireplace.*

PHOTO RIGHT: *If ever there were a reason to simply stay in bed, this is it — this gorgeous, twelve-foot stepped ceiling with recessed lighting is a sight to behold.*

PHOTO FAR RIGHT: *The master bath features a mammoth walk-in shower, step-up garden tub and generous "his" and "hers" walk-in closets.*

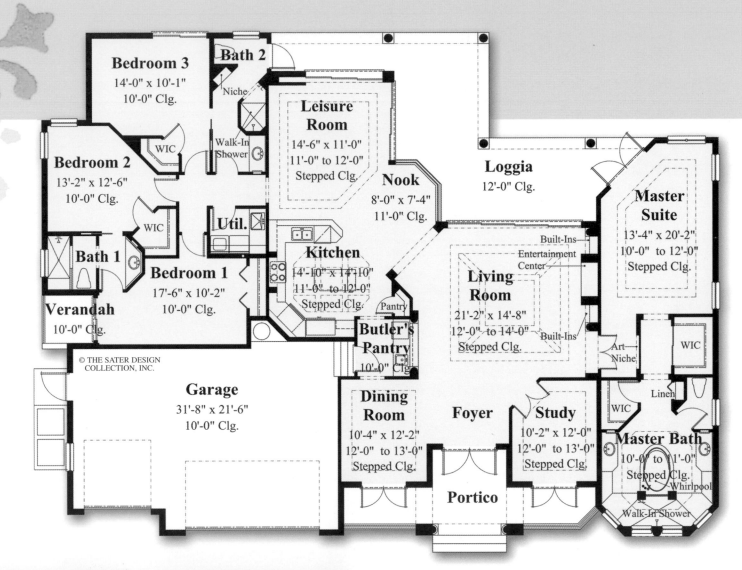

Bedroom 3
14'-0" x 10'-1"
10'-0" Clg.

Bath 2

Niche

Leisure Room
14'-6" x 11'-0"
11'-0" to 12'-0"
Stepped Clg.

Loggia
12'-0" Clg.

WIC

Walk-In Shower

Nook
8'-0" x 7'-4"
11'-0" Clg.

Master Suite
13'-4" x 20'-2"
10'-0" to 12'-0"
Stepped Clg.

Bedroom 2
13'-2" x 12'-6"
10'-0" Clg.

WIC

Util.

Kitchen
14'-10" x 14'-10"
11'-0" to 12'-0"
Stepped Clg.

Built-Ins

Entertainment Center

Bath 1

Bedroom 1
17'-6" x 10'-2"
10'-0" Clg.

Pantry

Living Room
21'-2" x 14'-8"
12'-0" to 14'-0"
Stepped Clg.

Built-Ins

WIC

Verandah
10'-0" Clg.

Butler's Pantry
10'-0" Clg.

Art Niche

WIC

Linen

© THE SATER DESIGN COLLECTION, INC.

Garage
31'-8" x 21'-6"
10'-0" Clg.

Dining Room
10'-4" x 12'-2"
12'-0" to 13'-0"
Stepped Clg.

Foyer

Study
10'-2" x 12'-0"
12'-0" to 13'-0"
Stepped Clg.

Master Bath
10'-0" to 11'-0"
Stepped Clg.
Whirlpool

Portico

Walk-In Shower

6778 | Deauville

4 Bedroom   Width: 80'10"

3 Bath   Depth: 59'10"

Living Area: **2,908 sq ft**

Exterior Walls: 8" CBS

Foundation: Slab

Price Code: **PSE5**

Sherbrooke

PHOTOGRAPHY BY: LAURENCE TAYLOR

PHOTO ABOVE: *This unique Mediterranean estate is nothing less than spectacular. True to its Revival roots — with just a touch of island vernacular — the façade boasts decorative columns, a recessed entry turret, low-pitched hipped roof and cupola. Just as impressive is the home's interior, where volume ceilings and walls of glass create nearly five-thousand square feet of luxurious livability.*

PHOTO RIGHT: *The design elements of the living room flow into the formal dining area in graceful arches, exotic columns with paneled fabric, and a high domed ceiling with exposed cypress beams.*

PHOTO ABOVE: *The living room, with access to the lanai via two sets of glass doors, is set apart from the dining and foyer area by Tuscan columns and made even more unique by an octagonal ceiling with inlaid wood. Attention to detail is evident in carved molding and majestic marble flooring.*

PHOTO LEFT: *An outdoor grill, at the far end of a rambling lanai, offers "serious" outdoor entertaining.*

PLAN | 6742

PHOTO ABOVE: *Topped with decorative corbels, an ornately carved partition wall separates the Roman tub from a spacious walk-in shower designed for two. Arch-top windows amplify the garden.*

PHOTO RIGHT: *The gourmet kitchen combines state-of-the-art appliances and amenities — hooded range, double ovens, food-preparation center island and marble counter tops — with casual comfort.*

PHOTO FAR RIGHT: *The leisure room is the perfect play place for adults with its built-in entertainment center, wet bar and nearby kitchen.*

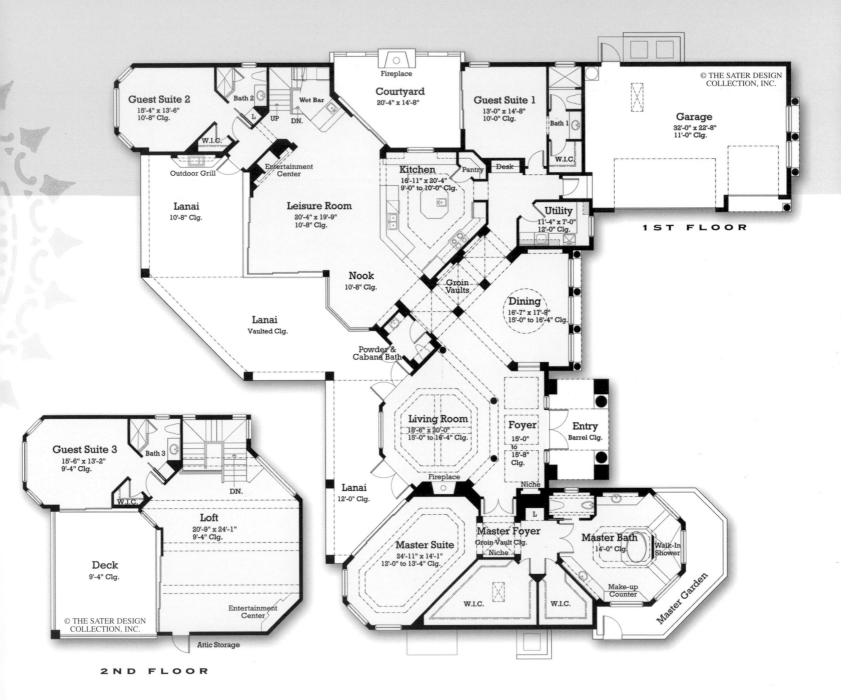

Fireplace

Guest Suite 2
15'-4" x 13'-6"
10'-8" Clg.

Bath 2

Wet Bar

Courtyard
20'-4" x 14'-8"

Guest Suite 1
13'-0" x 14'-8"
10'-0" Clg.

Bath 1

© THE SATER DESIGN
COLLECTION, INC.

Garage
32'-0" x 22'-8"
11'-0" Clg.

W.I.C.

W.I.C.

Outdoor Grill

Entertainment Center

Kitchen
16'-11" x 20'-4"
9'-0" to 10'-0" Clg.

Pantry

Desk

Lanai
10'-8" Clg.

Leisure Room
20'-4" x 19'-9"
10'-8" Clg.

Utility
11'-4" x 7'-0"
12'-0" Clg.

1ST FLOOR

Nook
10'-8" Clg.

Groin Vaults

Dining
16'-7" x 17'-9"
15'-0" to 16'-4" Clg.

Lanai
Vaulted Clg.

Powder & Cabana Bath

Living Room
18'-6" x 20'-0"
15'-0" to 16'-4" Clg.

Foyer
15'-0" to 15'-8" Clg.

Entry
Barrel Clg.

Guest Suite 3
15'-6" x 13'-2"
9'-4" Clg.

Bath 3

Niche

Fireplace

Lanai
12'-0" Clg.

Master Foyer
Groin Vault Clg.
Niche

Master Bath
14'-0" Clg.

Walk-In Shower

W.I.C.

DN.

Deck
9'-4" Clg.

Loft
20'-9" x 24'-1"
9'-4" Clg.

Master Suite
24'-11" x 14'-1"
12'-0" to 13'-4" Clg.

W.I.C.

W.I.C.

Make-up Counter

Master Garden

© THE SATER DESIGN
COLLECTION, INC.

Entertainment Center

Attic Storage

2ND FLOOR

6742 | Sherbrooke

4 Bedroom   Width: 91'4"
4-1/2 Bath   Depth: 109'0"
1st Floor: **3,933 sq ft**
2nd Floor: **838 sq ft**
Living Area: **4,771 sq ft**
Exterior Walls: 8" CBS
Foundation: Slab
Price Code: **PSE5**

PHOTOGRAPHY MAY DIFFER FROM BLUEPRINT.

NOT AVAILABLE FOR CONSTRUCTION IN

LEE OR COLLIER COUNTIES, FLORIDA.

Huntington Lakes

PHOTOGRAPHY BY: EVERETT & SOULÉ

PHOTO ABOVE: *Like a cat stretching out in his favorite sunny spot, this eye-catching Mediterranean home just basks in the sun, settling comfortably into its tropical surroundings. An elegant porte-cochere and stylish barrel dormer add touches of lavishness, but the home still retains its easy-going disposition.*

PHOTO RIGHT: *The formal dining room, with its opulent, octagonal step ceiling, boasts an adjacent wet bar and ample natural light from a trio of front-facing bay windows.*

PHOTO ABOVE: *If the rear elevation appears to be one continuous wraparound lanai, ample enough to accommodate a wedding party, that's because it is: almost two-thousand square feet in total.*

PHOTO LEFT: *Don't let the casual comfort of this kitchen fool you. It offers the serious chef every state-of-the-art food preparation amenity under the sun, and boasts fabulous details like the stone backsplash and hood.*

PHOTO ABOVE: *Reminiscent of an ancient pyramid, a great, carved-stone fireplace with tapered chimney warms this spacious living room. Complementing the massive hearth is a pair of stone Tuscan columns, stoically bearing the burden of a weighty arch.*

PHOTO RIGHT: *This cozy fireplace sitting area and impeccable outdoor kitchen are conveniently located just outside the guest suite.*

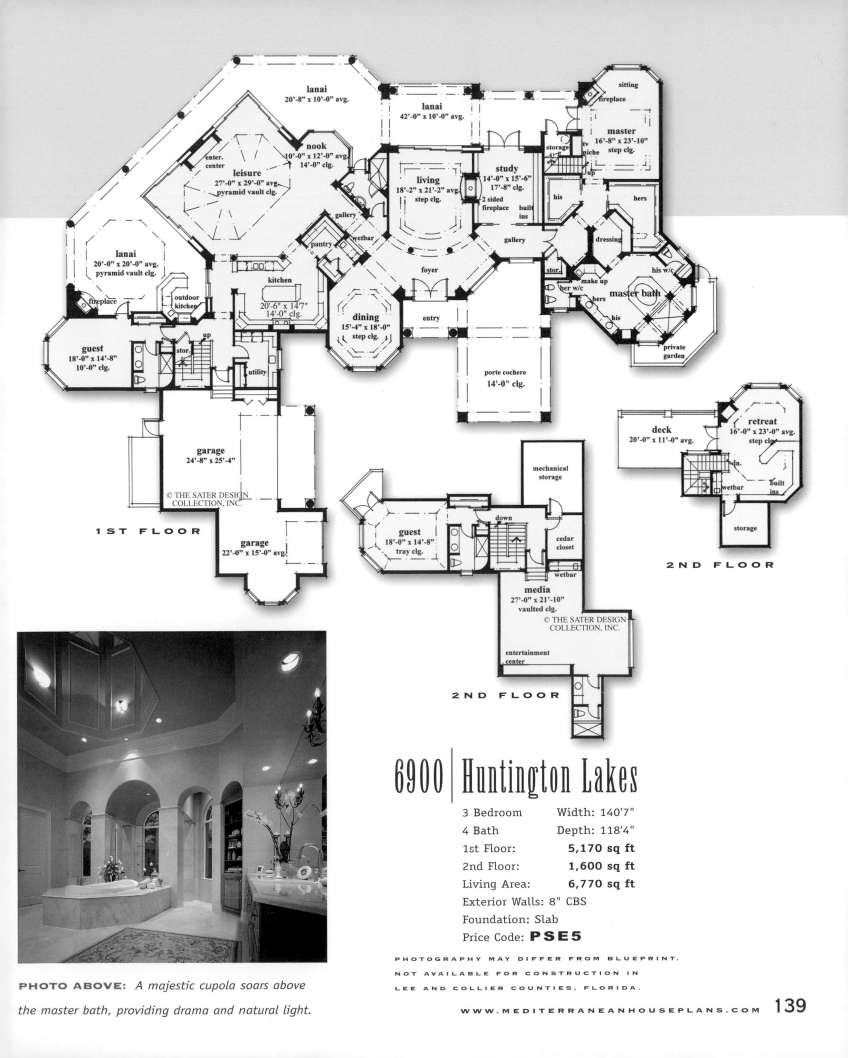

1ST FLOOR

lanai
20'-8" x 10'-0" avg.

lanai
42'-0" x 10'-0" avg.

sitting
fireplace

master
16'-8" x 23'-10"
step clg.

tv
niche

up

nook
10'-0" x 12'-0" avg.
14'-0" clg.

enter.
center

leisure
27'-0" x 29'-0" avg.
pyramid vault clg.

storage

study
14'-0" x 15'-6"
17'-8" clg.

living
18'-2" x 21'-2" avg.
step clg.

his

hers

2 sided
fireplace

built
ins

gallery

dressing

wetbar

gallery

his w/c

lanai
20'-0" x 20'-0" avg.
pyramid vault clg.

pantry

foyer

stor.

make up
her w/c

his

master bath

fireplace

outdoor
kitchen

kitchen
20'-6" x 14'7"
14'-0" clg.

dining
15'-4" x 18'-0"
step clg.

entry

hers

his

private
garden

guest
18'-0" x 14'-8"
10'-0" clg.

up

stor.

utility

porte cochere
14'-0" clg.

© THE SATER DESIGN
COLLECTION, INC.

garage
24'-8" x 25'-4"

garage
22'-0" x 15'-0" avg.

2ND FLOOR

deck
20'-0" x 11'-0" avg.

retreat
16'-0" x 23'-0" avg.
step clg.

dn.

wetbar

built
ins

storage

mechanical
storage

down

guest
18'-0" x 14'-8"
tray clg.

cedar
closet

wetbar

media
27'-0" x 21'-10"
vaulted clg.

© THE SATER DESIGN
COLLECTION, INC.

entertainment
center

2ND FLOOR

6900 | Huntington Lakes

3 Bedroom	Width: 140'7"
4 Bath	Depth: 118'4"
1st Floor:	**5,170 sq ft**
2nd Floor:	**1,600 sq ft**
Living Area:	**6,770 sq ft**

Exterior Walls: 8" CBS

Foundation: Slab

Price Code: **PSE5**

PHOTO ABOVE: *A majestic cupola soars above the master bath, providing drama and natural light.*

Monticello

PHOTOGRAPHY BY: LAURENCE TAYLOR

PHOTO ABOVE: A richly stated, recessed entry serves as both grand welcome and focal point for the façade of this contemporary Mediterranean-style resort home. Decorative columns stand guard on either side of this classic approach, leading to a set of mile-high double doors.

PHOTO RIGHT: Carved entry doors and an ornate barrel-vault ceiling are hallmarks of this stately, Moorish-influenced foyer.

PHOTO ABOVE: *Elegant-yet-sturdy ten-foot columns support soft slump arches, loosely defining the living room and generous dining room beyond. To the right, the grotto awaits behind two sets of wrought-iron gates.*

PHOTO LEFT: *The oval garden tub of the master bath, with its private view of the master garden, promises restoration and rejuvenation.*

PHOTO ABOVE: *Nook, leisure room and kitchen converge to create a spacious — and gracious — living area. Courtesy of zero-corner glass doors, spectacular exterior vistas become part of the equally spectacular interior landscape.*

PHOTO RIGHT: *Like sentries, statuesque columns stand guard at the boundary between indoor and outdoor spaces. An outdoor kitchen (visible to left) is just outside the leisure room, and offers a great place to gather for snacks and drinks.*

PHOTO FAR RIGHT: *The grotto makes a wonderful wine cellar. A unique groin-vaulted ceiling and wrought-iron gates create an ideal "temporary resting place" for favorite vintages.*

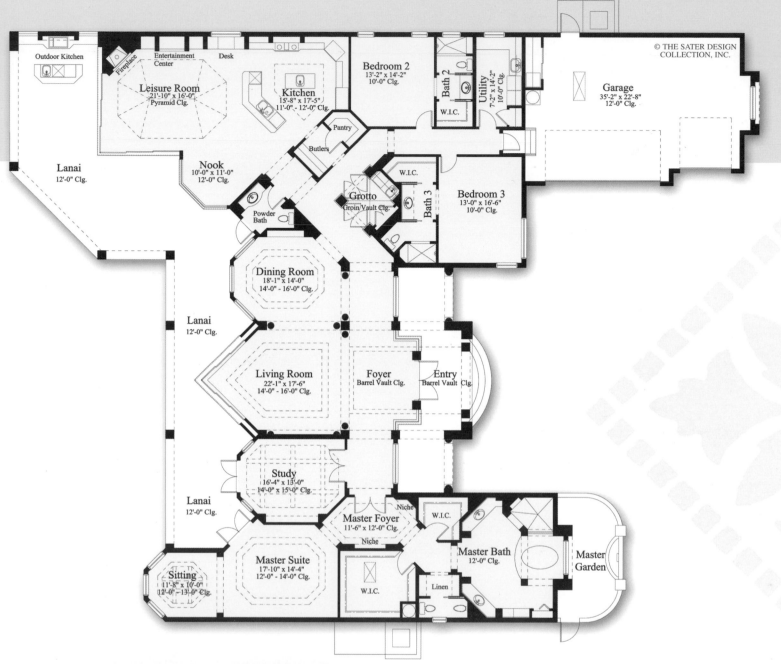

Outdoor Kitchen

Fireplace

Entertainment Center

Desk

Leisure Room
21'-10" x 16'-0"
Pyramid Clg.

Kitchen
15'-8" x 17'-5"
11'-0" - 12'-0" Clg.

Bedroom 2
13'-2" x 14'-2"
10'-0" Clg.

Bath 2

Utility
7'-2" x 14'-2"
10'-0" Clg.

Garage
35'-2" x 22'-8"
12'-0" Clg.

© THE SATER DESIGN COLLECTION, INC.

W.I.C.

Lanai
12'-0" Clg.

Nook
10'-0" x 11'-0"
12'-0" Clg.

Pantry

Butlers

Grotto
Groin/Vault Clg.

W.I.C.

Bath 3

Bedroom 3
13'-0" x 16'-6"
10'-0" Clg.

Powder Bath

Dining Room
18'-1" x 14'-0"
14'-0" - 16'-0" Clg.

Lanai
12'-0" Clg.

Living Room
22'-1" x 17'-6"
14'-0" - 16'-0" Clg.

Foyer
Barrel Vault Clg.

Entry
Barrel Vault Clg.

Lanai
12'-0" Clg.

Study
16'-4" x 13'-0"
14'-0" - 15'-0" Clg.

Niche

W.I.C.

Master Foyer
11'-6" x 12'-0" Clg.

Niche

Master Bath
12'-0" Clg.

Master Garden

Sitting
11'-8" x 10'-0"
12'-0" - 13'-0" Clg.

Master Suite
17'-10" x 14'-4"
12'-0" - 14'-0" Clg.

W.I.C.

Linen

6907 | Monticello

3 Bedroom	Width: 91'6"
3-1/2 Bath	Depth: 117'0"
Living Area:	**4,255 sq ft**

Exterior Walls: 8" CBS

Foundation: Slab

Price Code: **PSE5**

WWW.MEDITERRANEANHOUSEPLANS.COM

Starwood

PHOTOGRAPHY BY: LAURENCE TAYLOR

PHOTO ABOVE: *The repetition of graceful arches and elegant columns presents an elegant façade for this stately Mediterranean-inspired home.*

PHOTO RIGHT: *In the study, high timber beams repeat a natural theme expressed below by maple floors and a wood-trimmed mantle.*

PHOTO FAR RIGHT: *An air of serenity prevails throughout the neo-Mediterranean interior, expressed perfectly in the living room. Floor-to-ceiling glass permits nature to intrude, and grants spacious views of the veranda.*

PLAN | 6911

PHOTO ABOVE: *An open foyer eases the transition from the outdoors to the elegant living and dining rooms, which are suffused with natural light.*

PHOTO RIGHT: *Sand-hued cabinets and counter tops subdue a seamless bay window that permits views of a lush private garden outside the master bath.*

PHOTO FAR RIGHT: *A covered veranda rambles freely along the rear of this home, providing areas for intimate conversations or large gatherings.*

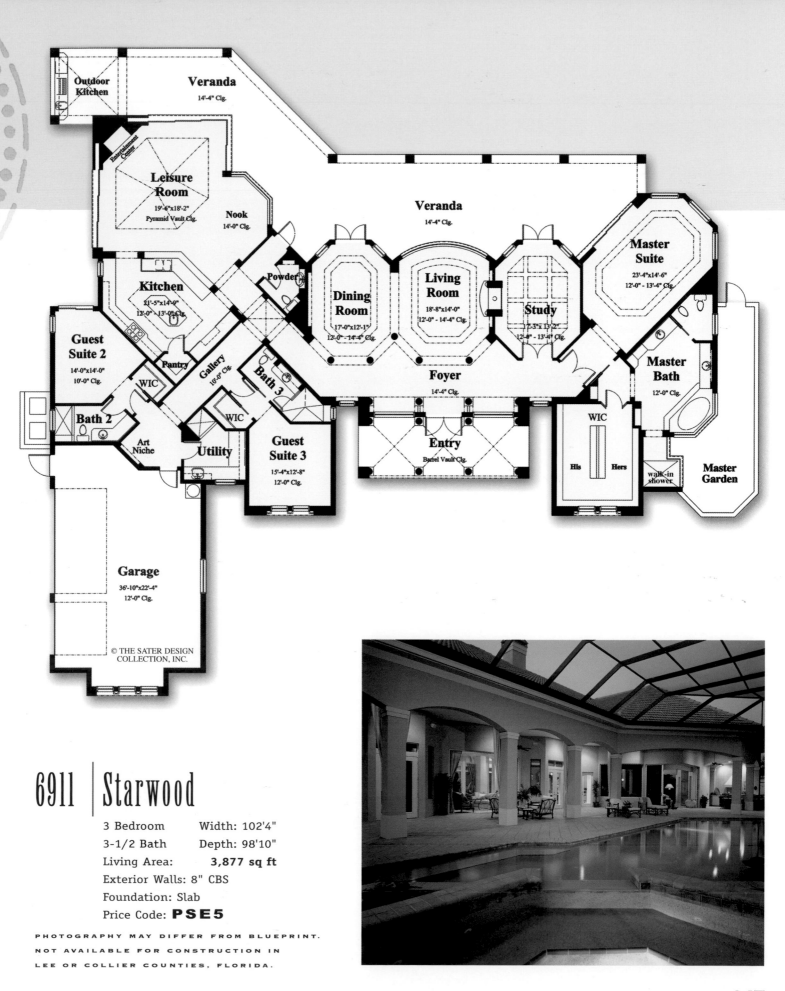

Outdoor Kitchen

Veranda
14'-4" Clg.

Leisure Room
19'-6"x18'-2"
Pyramid Vault Clg.

Nook
14'-0" Clg.

Entertainment Center

Veranda
14'-4" Clg.

Master Suite
23'-4"x14'-6"
12'-0" - 13'-4" Clg.

Kitchen
21'-5"x14'-9"
12'-0" - 13'-0" Clg.

Powder

Dining Room
17'-0"x12'-1"
12'-0" - 14'-4" Clg.

Living Room
18'-8"x14'-0"
12'-0" - 14'-4" Clg.

Study
17'-3"x13'-2"
12'-0" - 13'-4" Clg.

Guest Suite 2
14'-0"x14'-0"
10'-0" Clg.

Pantry

WIC

Gallery
10'-0" Clg.

Bath 3

WIC

Foyer
14'-4" Clg.

Master Bath
12'-0" Clg.

Bath 2

Art Niche

Utility

Guest Suite 3
15'-4"x12'-8"
12'-0" Clg.

Entry
Barrel Vault Clg.

WIC

His   **Hers**

walk-in shower

Master Garden

Garage
36'-10"x22'-4"
12'-0" Clg.

© THE SATER DESIGN COLLECTION, INC.

6911 | Starwood

3 Bedroom   Width: 102'4"
3-1/2 Bath   Depth: 98'10"
Living Area: **3,877 sq ft**
Exterior Walls: 8" CBS
Foundation: Slab
Price Code: **PSE5**

PHOTOGRAPHY MAY DIFFER FROM BLUEPRINT.
NOT AVAILABLE FOR CONSTRUCTION IN
LEE OR COLLIER COUNTIES, FLORIDA.

Broadmoor Walk

PHOTOGRAPHY BY: OSCAR THOMPSON

PHOTO ABOVE: *Stately columns support a lovely arched entry with a dramatic bayed turret by its side. This attractive, contemporary-style villa stretches out beneath a turquoise sky. Its interior invites the outside in via a myriad of windows and five sets of double doors.*

PHOTO RIGHT: *Mirrored in a tranquil pool, this spectacular covered loggia — with its graceful arches and statuesque column design — brings an unparalleled opulence to outdoor entertaining. Three sets of elegant French doors provide access from the common area shared by the living and dining rooms.*

2ND FLOOR

1ST FLOOR

Master Sitting
12'-0" x 14'-3"
12'-0" Tray Clg.

Fireplace — Morning Kitchen

Master Suite
17'-0" x 20'-8"
12'-0" Tray Clg.

Loggia

Whirlpool

W.I.C.

W.I.C.

Master Bath
Tray Clg.

Glass Block Shower

Built-Ins

Personal Valet

Wet Bar

Gallery

Grand Hall
13'-0" Clg.

Gallery

Pwdr. Bath

Library
12'-8" x 15'-8"
13'-4" Clg.

Entry

Built-Ins

Living Room
20'-8" x 16'-8"
13'-4" Clg.

Dining Room
9'-0" x 16'-8"
13'-4" Clg.

Fireplace

Loggia
12'-0" Clg.

Outdoor Kichen

Leisure Room
17'-8" x 22'-8"
12'-0" Clg.

Pool Bath

Entertainment Center

Nook
9'-5" x 13'-1"
12'-0" Clg.

Kitchen
18'-4" x 17'-0"

Built-Ins

Pantry

Powder Bath

Bath #2

Guest Suite 2
15'-4" x 12'-8"
9'-4" Clg.

Bath #3

Guest Suite 3
13'-0" x 13'-0"
9'-4" Clg.

DryAire

Iron Station

Studio

9'-4"x7'-8" SinkSpa Duet W/D

W.I.C.

Planter

Planter

Garage
22'-8" x 35'-0"

Attic Space

Dormer

Bonus Room
9'-0" x 28'-0"

Dormer

Down

© THE SATER DESIGN COLLECTION, INC.

© THE SATER DESIGN COLLECTION, INC.

6641 | Broadmoor Walk

3 Bedroom	Width: 90'0"
4 Full, 2 Half Baths	Depth: 128'8"
1st Floor:	**3,896 sq ft**
Living Area:	**3,896 sq ft**
Bonus Room:	**356 sq ft**
Exterior Walls: 8" CBS or 2x6	
Foundation: Slab	
Price Code: **L1**	

PHOTO ABOVE: *Breezes cool the living room through sliding doors and are then warmed by a fire blazing in this majestic fireplace.*

PHOTOGRAPHY MAY DIFFER FROM BLUEPRINT.

Illustrated Designs

These beautifully rendered plans articulate Mediterranean

design loud and clear. Spanish, Tuscan and

Moorish influences throughout highlight soaring ceilings with

striking treatments, dramatic arched windows and

disappearing walls that flood rooms with fresh air

and light. Also included are stunning

state-of-the-art kitchens, fabulous master

suites with over-the-top amenities, and outdoor areas

that offer first-class relaxing

and entertaining.

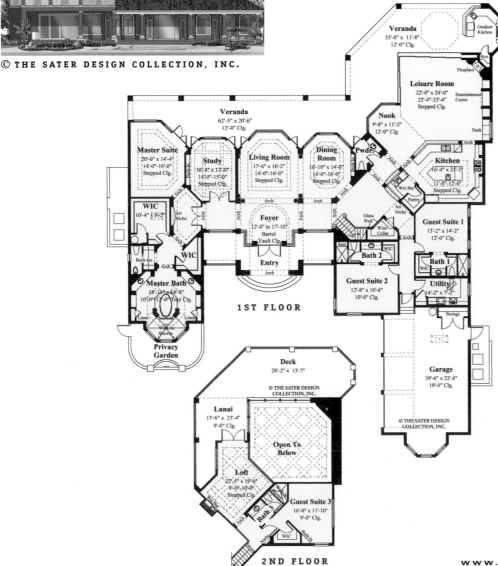

REAR ELEVATION

© THE SATER DESIGN COLLECTION, INC.

La Ventana

Rope molding adds flair to the Moorish-style entry in this detail-rich Mediterranean manor. The foyer is grand under a barrel-vault ceiling and leads to a living room walled in glass along the back. The guest suites and family spaces are to the right, with the leisure room opening to a veranda and an outdoor kitchen. The master suite is commanding with a stepped ceiling, two walk-in closets and a luxurious bath where a centered tub "floats" under a tray ceiling. The second level offers a private guest suite, complete with a loft and wrapping deck.

4 Bedroom

4-1/2 Bath

Width: 101'4"

Depth: 120'8"

1st Floor: **4,369 sq ft**

2nd Floor: **640 sq ft**

Living Area: **5,009 sq ft**

Exterior Walls: 8" CBS

Foundation: Slab

Price Code: **PSE5**

Salcito

This enchanting courtyard home features private, family and guest spaces filled with Mediterranean design details and open connections to a central loggia with fountain pool. The second level includes a study, two bedroom suites and multiple decks with courtyard views. The main-floor leisure room has a two-story boxed-beamed ceiling, a wall of built-ins, and a wall of glass doors to the loggia.

4 Bedroom

4-1/2 Bath

Width: 45'0" Bldg./52'2" w/Garden

Depth: 94'0"

1st Floor: **2,357 sq ft**

2nd Floor: **1,116 sq ft**

Living Area: **3,473 sq ft**

Exterior Walls: 8" CBS or 2x6

Foundation: Slab

Price Code: **C4**

1ST FLOOR

2ND FLOOR

INTERIOR COURTYARD

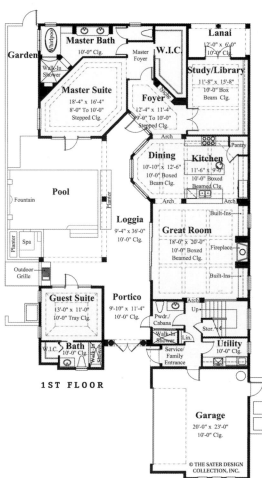

Ferretti

Arched iron gates in the portico offer regal entry to a fabulous secluded courtyard. Rooms surround a pool and fountain with lots of glass for seamless indoor-outdoor living. A second floor features two guest suites and a loft, plus a balcony and deck that offer views of the courtyard from two different perspectives. The master suite has an elegant foyer and a private garden.

4 Bedroom

5 Bath

Width: 44'10" Bldg./52'0" w/Garden

Depth: 95'8"

1st Floor: **2,011 sq ft**

2nd Floor: **777 sq ft**

Guest Suite: **243 sq ft**

Living Area: **3,031 sq ft**

Exterior Walls: 8" CBS or 2x6

Foundation: Slab

Price Code: **C4**

2ND FLOOR

© THE SATER DESIGN COLLECTION, INC.

Deck 9'-8" x 11'-10"

Balcony 18'-0" x 5'-0"

Loft 10'-0" x 16'-4" 9'-4" Stepped Clg.

Guest Suite 3 13'-0" x 11'-0" 9'-4" Stepped Clg.

Bath 9'-4" Clg.

Balconette

Bath 9'-4" Clg.

Down

Guest Suite 2 13'-4" x 13'-4" 9'-4" Stepped Clg.

W.I.C.

1ST FLOOR

© THE SATER DESIGN COLLECTION, INC.

Garden

Master Bath 10'-0" Clg.

Whirlpool

Walk-In Shower

Master Foyer

W.I.C.

Lanai 12'-0" x 6'-0" 10'-0" Clg.

Study/Library 11'-8" x 15'-8" 10'-0" Box Beam Clg.

Master Suite 18'-4" x 16'-4" 8'-0" To 10'-0" Stepped Clg.

Foyer 12'-4" x 11'-4" 9'-9" To 10'-0" Stepped Clg.

Arch

Pool

Fountain

Planter

Loggia 9'-4" x 36'-0" 10'-0" Clg.

Arch

Dining 10'-10" x 12'-6" 10'-0" Boxed Beam Clg.

Kitchen 11'-6" x 9'-0" 10'-0" Boxed Beamed Clg.

Pantry

Arch

Great Room 18'-0" x 20'-0" 10'-0" Boxed Beamed Clg.

Built-Ins

Fireplace

Built-Ins

Planter

Spa

Outdoor Grille

Guest Suite 13'-0" x 11'-0" 10'-0" Tray Clg.

Portico 9'-10" x 11'-4" 10'-0" Clg.

Pwdr./ Cabana

Arch

Up

Walk-In Shower

Bath 10'-0" Clg.

W.I.C.

Lin.

Service/ Family Entrance

Stor.

Utility 10'-0" Clg.

Garage 20'-0" x 23'-0" 10'-0" Clg.

INTERIOR COURTYARD

REAR ELEVATION

© THE SATER DESIGN COLLECTION, INC.

Napier

A unique two-story master suite makes this home fabulous. The bedroom and spectacular bath with private garden are downstairs; a den, exercise room, half-bath and deck are above. Across the home, another second-level space includes a full bedroom suite with deck, plus a media room or fourth bedroom also with a private bath and balcony. The main floor has every amenity imaginable in rooms that merge with wraparound outdoor spaces.

4 Bedroom

5-1/2 Bath

Width: 145'4"

Depth: 116'10"

1st Floor: **5,155 sq ft**

2nd Floor: **1,700 sq ft**

Living Area: **6,855 sq ft**

Exterior Walls: 8" CBS

Foundation: Slab

Price Code: **PSE5**

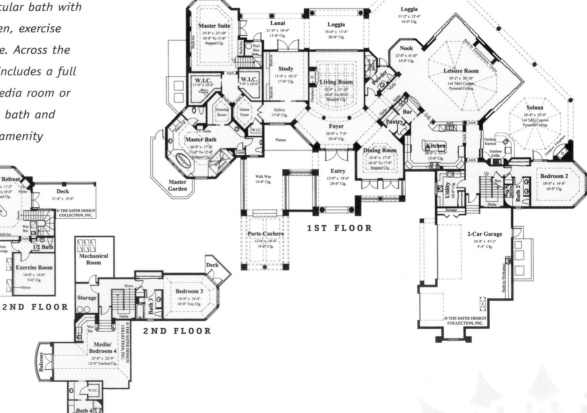

NOT AVAILABLE FOR CONSTRUCTION IN LEE OR COLLIER COUNTIES, FLORIDA.

REAR ELEVATION

© THE SATER DESIGN COLLECTION, INC.

Rosario

Arches and Tuscan columns make a bold Mediterranean statement. Inside, a smart floor plan loaded with windows and walls of glass enhance both indoor and outdoor living. The masterpiece is the center living and dining rooms divided by a floating bar and bordered by pocketing glass walls to the lanai. The secluded master retreat occupies an entire side of the home.

3 Bedroom

3-1/2 Bath

Width: 65'0"

Depth: 90'6"

Living Area: **3,184 sq ft**

Exterior Walls: 8" CBS or 2x6

Foundation: Slab

Price Code: **C 4**

Built-Ins

Leisure Room
17'-0" x 20'-5"
10'-0" - 11'-0"
Stepped Clg.

Nook
8'-4" x 10'-10"
10'-0" Clg.

Lanai
10'-0" Clg.

Master Suite
14'-2" x 19'-8"
10'-0" - 11'-0"
Stepped Clg.

Kitchen
12'-0" x 17'-6"
10'-0" Clg.

Desk

Butler's Pantry

Floating Bar

WIC

Dining Room
12'-1" x 15'-4"
13'-0" - 14'-0"
Stepped Clg.

Living Room
15'-10" x 15'-4"
13'-0" - 14'-0"
Stepped Clg.

Built-Ins

Pwdr.

Pantry

Bath 3
10'-0" Clg.

Art Niche

Arch

Bath 2
10'-0" Clg.

Foyer
13'-0" Clg.

Master Bath
10'-0" Clg.

Tub

Bedroom 3
11'-8" x 12'-0"
10'-0" Clg.

Cl.

Entry
14'-0" Clg.

Study
9'-8" x 16'-3"
13'-0" - 14'-0"
Stepped Clg.

Walk-In Shower

Master Garden

Bedroom 2
11'-2" x 13'-6"
10'-0" Clg.

Utility
10'-0" Clg.

Work Bench

2-Car Garage
21'-8" x 21'-2"
10'-0" Clg.

© THE SATER DESIGN COLLECTION, INC.

Arch

REAR ELEVATION

© THE SATER DESIGN COLLECTION, INC.

La Posada

Decorative pendants add one-of-a-kind detail to the entryway cornice. Inside, the living room, kitchen and leisure room flow together and offer uninterrupted access and views to the lanai through disappearing glass walls and mitered windows. An island and large walk-in pantry make the kitchen sparkle. Owners will enjoy privacy in a master suite tucked to one side of the home.

4 Bedroom

3 Bath

Width: 60'4"

Depth: 78'9"

Living Area: **2,554 sq ft**

Exterior Walls: **8" CBS or 2x6**

Foundation: Slab

Price Code: **C3**

Bath 3

Leisure Room
17'-3" x 15'-8"
10'-0" to 11'-0"
Stepped Clg.

Entertainment Center

Bedroom 4
11'-8" x 11'-0"
10'-0" Clg.

Nook
5'-6" x 8'-6"
10'-0" Clg.

Lanai
26'-2" x 9'-4"
10'-0" Clg.

Kitchen
10'-0" to 11'-0"
Stepped Clg.

Bedroom 3
11'-0" x 11'-0"
10'-0" Clg.

Pantry

Living Room
16'-3" x 15'-2"
12'-0" to 13'-0"
Stepped Clg.

Master Suite
16'-7" x 14'-0"
10'-0" to 12'-0"
Tray Clg.

Art Niches

Bath 2

Niche

Arch

Arch

Dining Room
11'-8" x 10'-2"
11'-0" to 12'-0"
Stepped Clg.

Utility
10'-0" Clg.

Bedroom 2
11'-8" x 13'-4"
10'-0" Clg.

Foyer

W.I.C.

Niche

Master Bath
9'-0" x 15'-2"
10'-0" Clg.

Built-ins

Entry

Storage

Garage
20'-8" x 24'-2"
11'-4" Clg.

© THE SATER DESIGN COLLECTION, INC.

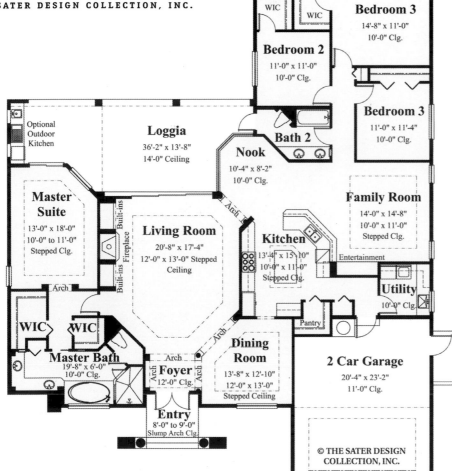

REAR ELEVATION

Esperane

A slump-arch ceiling defines the elegant entryway into this Mediterranean family home. The living room is charming, with a fireplace surrounded by built-ins and disappearing glass walls to the loggia. The nearby kitchen, nook and leisure room make this floor plan ideal for both entertaining and family living. The master suite gets lots of privacy and space, as well as a luxurious bathroom.

4 Bedroom

2 Bath

Width: 63'8"

Depth: 72'8"

Living Area: **2,654 sq ft**

Exterior Walls: 8" CBS

Foundation: Slab

Price Code: **C 3**

Floor plan labels:

Optional Outdoor Kitchen

Loggia 36'-2" x 13'-8" 14'-0" Ceiling

WIC

WIC

Bedroom 2 11'-0" x 11'-0" 10'-0" Clg.

Bedroom 3 14'-8" x 11'-0" 10'-0" Clg.

Bath 2

Nook 10'-4" x 8'-2" 10'-0" Clg.

Bedroom 3 11'-0" x 11'-4" 10'-0" Clg.

Master Suite 13'-0" x 18'-0" 10'-0" to 11'-0" Stepped Clg.

Built-ins Fireplace Built-ins

Living Room 20'-8" x 17'-4" 12'-0" x 13'-0" Stepped Ceiling

Kitchen 13'-4" x 15'-10" 10'-0" x 11'-0" Stepped Clg.

Family Room 14'-0" x 14'-8" 10'-0" x 11'-0" Stepped Clg.

Entertainment

Arch

WIC WIC

Master Bath 19'-8" x 6'-0" 10'-0" Clg.

Arch Foyer 12'-0" Clg.

Arch Arch

Dining Room 13'-8" x 12'-10" 12'-0" x 13'-0" Stepped Ceiling

Pantry

Utility 10'-0" Clg.

2 Car Garage 20'-4" x 23'-2" 11'-0" Clg.

Entry 8'-0" to 9'-0" Slump Arch Clg.

REAR ELEVATION

© THE SATER DESIGN COLLECTION, INC.

Bartolini

Corbels, balustrades and detailed window treatments make this Italian Renaissance home look stunning from the street. As functional on the inside as it is stylish on the exterior, this wonderful floor plan is centralized around an extraordinary courtyard. The rear-entry garage has a large bonus room or guest suite with circular staircase above that overlooks the garden area below.

3 Bedroom

2-1/2 Bath

Width: 60'6"

Depth: 94'0"

1st Floor: **2,084 sq ft**

2nd Floor: **652 sq ft**

Living Area: **2,736 sq ft**

Bonus Room: **375 sq ft**

Exterior Walls: 2x6

Foundation: Slab or Optional Basement

Price Code: **C3**

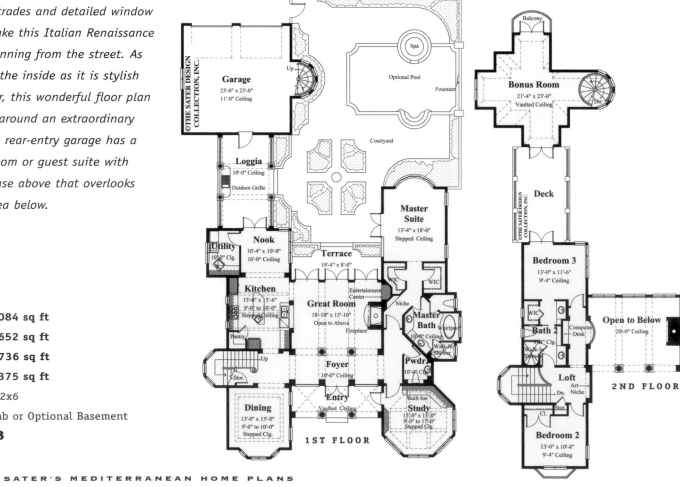

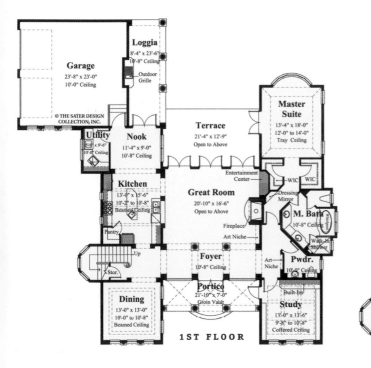

REAR ELEVATION

© THE SATER DESIGN COLLECTION, INC.

Corsini

Triple French doors deck out the façade, adding light to the front of the home and establishing a striking street presence. A lateral arrangement of the kitchen, loggia, morning nook and formal dining room eases the service of meals, from planned events with hors d'oeuvres alfresco to grilling parties by the pool. The upper level provides a gallery loft that grants interior vistas through the great room, and connects four secondary bedrooms — one with a private deck — that share two baths.

1ST FLOOR

Garage
23'-8" x 23'-0"
10'-0" Ceiling

© THE SATER COLLECTION, INC.

Loggia
8'-4" x 23'-6"
10'-8" Ceiling
Outdoor Grille

Utility
9'-6"
10'-4" Ceiling

Nook
11'-4" x 9'-0"
10'-8" Ceiling

Terrace
21'-4" x 12'-9"
Open to Above

Master Suite
13'-4" x 18'-0"
12'-0" to 14'-0"
Tray Ceiling

Kitchen
13'-0" x 5'-6"
10'-2" to 10'-8"
Beamed Ceiling

Pantry

Great Room
20'-10" x 16'-6"
Open to Above

Entertainment Center

WIC   WIC

Dressing Mirror

M. Bath
10'-8" Ceiling

Whirlpool

Fireplace

Art Niche

Walk-In Shower

Foyer
10'-8" Ceiling

Up

Stor.

Art Niche

Pwdr.
10'-0" Ceiling

Dining
13'-0" x 13'-0"
10'-0" to 10'-8"
Beamed Ceiling

Portico
21'-10" x 7'-0"
Groin Vault

Built-Ins

Study
13'-0" x 13'-6"
9'-8" to 10'-8"
Coffered Ceiling

2ND FLOOR

Sun Deck

Bedroom 3
13'-0" x 11'-6"
9'-4" Ceiling

WIC

Bath 2
9'-4" Clg

Walk-In Shower

Computer Desk

© THE SATER DESIGN COLLECTION, INC.

Open to Below
23'-0" to 24'-0"
Beamed Ceiling

Bedroom 5
13'-0" x 14'-0"
9'-4" Ceiling
Window Seat

Loft
9'-4" Clg.

Dn.

Stor.

Bedroom 2
13'-0" x 11'-1"
9'-4" Ceiling

Balcony
8'-6" Clg.

Walk-In Shower   Bath 3
9'-4" Clg.

WIC

Bedroom 4
13'-0" x 11'-1"
9'-4" Ceiling

5 Bedroom
3-1/2 Bath
Width: 71'0"
Depth: 72'0"
1st Floor: **2,163 sq ft**
2nd Floor: **1,415 sq ft**
Living Area: **3,578 sq ft**
Exterior Walls: 2x6
Foundation: Slab or Optional Basement
Price Code: **L1**

Laparelli

Arch-top windows bring natural light into the formal spaces, while retreating walls along the lanai extend both public and private realms beyond the home's footprint. Well-organized and equipped for sophisticated gatherings, the kitchen serves the formal dining room via a gallery, while a wet bar and cabana bath announce the casual living space. The owners' retreat provides a magnificent bedroom with a sitting bay and morning kitchen. Capture the moonlight and stars through private access to the wraparound lanai.

3 Bedroom

4 Bath

Width: 83'10"

Depth: 106'0"

Living Area: **3,942 sq ft**

Exterior Walls: 2x6

Foundation: Slab

Price Code: **L1**

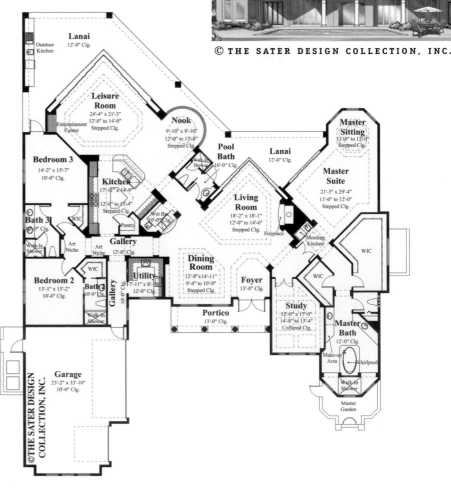

REAR ELEVATION

© THE SATER DESIGN COLLECTION, INC.

REAR ELEVATION

© THE SATER DESIGN COLLECTION, INC.

Verrado

Stone balustrades create an entryway patio, making this home ultra-impressive. The interior impresses, too, with zero-corner pocket doors in the living room, a private master suite with a privacy garden, and a fabulous Solana with an outdoor grill and fireplace. The second floor offers two guest rooms with a shared bath, a bonus room with its own lanai and deck, and even a wet bar complete with a popcorn maker.

4 Bedroom

3-1/2 Bath

Width: 65'0"

Depth: 115'0"

1st Floor: **3,008 sq ft**

2nd Floor: **983 sq ft**

Living Area: **3,991 sq ft**

Exterior Walls: 8" CBS

Foundation: Slab

Price Code: **L1**

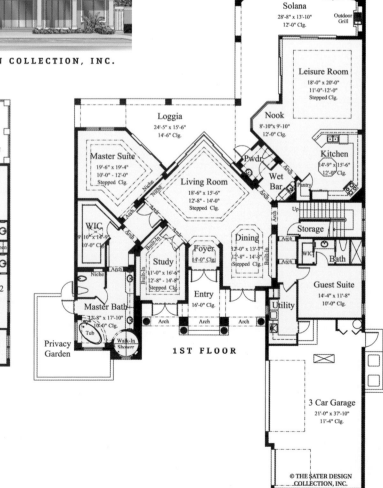

© THE SATER DESIGN COLLECTION, INC.

2ND FLOOR

1ST FLOOR

Bellini

Arches, columns and an enchanting series of decorative brackets define the perfect blend of old and new — and conceal an open interior layered with details. An open gallery and a sculpted arcade announce the living/dining room — a splendid space anchored by a massive fireplace. French doors invite the outdoors inside, where fresh breezes mingle with an authentic European temperament. Contemporary spaces reside in the private realm: a state-of-the-art kitchen overlooks a bumped-out morning nook and a media room with retreating walls.

3 Bedroom

2 Full, 2 Half Bath

Width: 84'0"

Depth: 92'2"

Living Area: **3,351 sq ft**

Exterior Walls: 2x6

Foundation: Slab

Price Code: **C4**

REAR ELEVATION

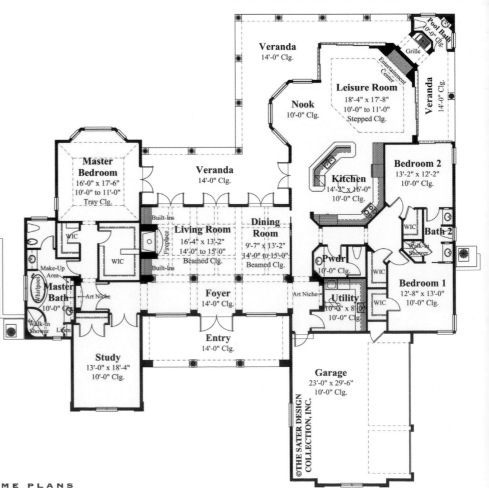

© THE SATER DESIGN COLLECTION, INC.

REAR ELEVATION

© THE SATER DESIGN COLLECTION, INC.

Martelli

An eye-catching turret highlights this Mediterranean-style elevation with its defining curb appeal. A recessed entry defines the finely detailed façade, and a quatrefoil window confirms a Moorish influence. Inside, an open arrangement of the foyer and the formal rooms permits natural light to flow freely through the space. Walls of glass to the rear of the plan open the interior to spectacular views.

4 Bedroom
3-1/2 Bath
Width: 68'8"
Depth: 91'8"
Living Area: **3,497 sq ft**
Exterior Walls: 2x6 or 8" CBS
Foundation: Slab
Price Code: **C4**

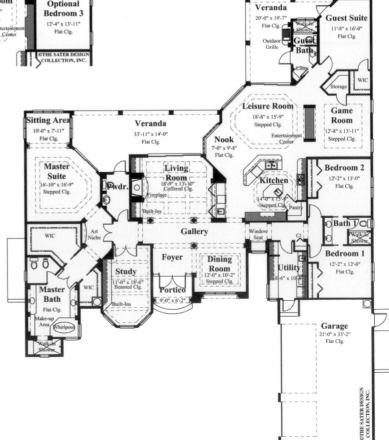

© THE SATER DESIGN COLLECTION, INC.

Salina

Hipped roof lines, carved eave brackets and stone accents evoke a sense of the past. An engaging blend of old and new prevails inside, where beamed and coffered ceilings play counterpoint to modern amenities — a wet bar, cutting-edge appliances in the gourmet kitchen, and a freestanding media center between the leisure and game rooms. Secluded to the rear of the plan, guest quarters include a cabana-style bath that opens to a separate veranda.

4 Bedroom

3-1/2 Bath

Width: 80'0"

Depth: 104'8"

Living Area: **3,743 sq ft**

Exterior Walls: 2x6

Foundation: Slab or Optional Basement

Price Code: **L1**

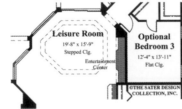

REAR ELEVATION

© THE SATER DESIGN COLLECTION, INC.

Balcony
10'-12" x 9'-4"

Grand Room
Beamed Clg.

Open to Below

Bedroom 2
10'-11" x 13'-4"
10'-0" Clg.

©THE SATER DESIGN COLLECTION, INC.

Open to Below

WIC

Bath 2
10'-0" Clg.

Bath 3

Balcony
10'-7" x 14'-4"

Bedroom 3
15'-0" x 11'-6"
10'-0" Clg.

WIC

WIC

Bedroom 4
11'-6" x 16'-8"
10'-0" Clg.

Balcony

2ND FLOOR

La Reina

The paneled portal opens to a portico and courtyard, which creates a procession to the formal entry of the home. To the front of the courtyard, a casita, or guest house, offers space that easily converts to a workshop or home office. The foyer opens directly to the grand room and, through an arched opening, to the formal dining room. Glass bayed walls in the central living area and study help meld inside and outside spaces.

5 Bedroom

4-1/2 Bath

Width: 80'0"

Depth: 96'0"

1st Floor: **2,852 sq ft**

2nd Floor: **969 sq ft**

Guest Suite: **330 sq ft**

Living Area: **4,151 sq ft**

Exterior Walls: 2x6

Foundation: Slab

Price Code: **L2**

Loggia
26'-10" x 11'-8"
Open to Above

Loggia
15'-6" x 10'-0"
10'-0" Clg.

Master Suite
14'-8" x 22'-4"
12'-0" to 14'-0"
Stepped Clg.

WIC

Whirlpool

M. Bath
12'-0" to 14'-0"
Stepped Clg.

WIC

Walk-In Shower

Linen

Grand Room
19'-0" x 19'-5"
Open to Above

Dining Room
10'-6" x 13'-4"
10'-0" Clg.

Pwdr.
9'-4" Clg.

Foyer

Up

Built-In Server

Utility
6'-8" x 9'-8"
10'-0" Clg.

Study
14'-4" x 15'-0"
12'-0" to 13'-0"
Stepped Clg.

Loggia
10'-0" Clg.

Desk

Nook
10'-0" Clg.

Kitchen
13'-8" x 15'-4"
10'-0" Clg.

Pantry

Fountain

Spa

Optional Pool

Courtyard

Loggia
16'-8" Clg.

Leisure Room
18'-6" x 17'-10"
10'-0" to 14'-6"
Stepped Clg.

Built-In Entertainment

Garage
11'-6" x 16'-10"
10'-0" Clg.

Fireplace

Loggia
10'-0" Clg.

Outdoor Kitchen

Guest Suite
14'-4" x 13'-5"
10'-0" Clg.

WIC

Pool Bath

Portico
14'-8" X 14'-4"
Groin Vault

©THE SATER DESIGN COLLECTION, INC.

Garage
22'-4" x 25'-6"
10'-0" Clg.

1ST FLOOR

Porta Rossa

Mediterranean low-pitched rooflines lend a sense of authenticity to the façade, while a carved entry extends a warm welcome. Interior vistas mix it up with sunlight and fresh breezes through the plan via sliding walls of glass that connect living spaces to the outdoors. The high-glam master suite boasts a step-up, spa-style tub, a garden wall and a frameless walk-in shower.

4 Bedroom

3-1/2 Bath

Width: 67'0"

Depth: 91'8"

Living Area: **3,166 sq ft**

Exterior Walls: 2x6

Foundation: Slab or 8" CBS

Price Code: **C4**

REAR ELEVATION

© THE SATER DESIGN COLLECTION, INC.

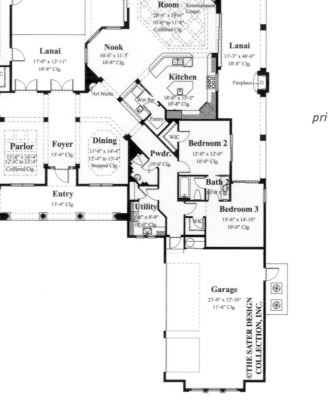

REAR ELEVATION

© THE SATER DESIGN COLLECTION, INC.

Caprina

Evocative of Spanish Colonial vernacular, this exquisite villa invites a reconnection to nature. Rows of arch-top windows and spiral pilasters enhance the sidewalk presence, while coffered ceilings and a no-walls approach to formal rooms provide an immediate sense of openness upon entry. A wraparound lanai connects public and private realms with an adjoining guest suite that is both comfortable and secluded.

4 Bedroom

3-1/2 Bath

Width: 74'8"

Depth: 118'0"

Guest Suite: **297 sq ft**

Living Area: **3,271 sq ft**

Exterior Walls: 2x6

Foundation: Slab

Price Code: **C4**

Raphaello

Arched windows and barrel-tiled roofs set off smooth, cast-stone elements with this splendid villa. Living spaces oriented to the rear of the plan take in views and natural light through great walls of glass that also grant access to the lanai. On the upper level, secondary bedrooms adjoin a compartmented bath and open to a shared deck.

3 Bedroom

3-1/2 Bath

Width: 72'0"

Depth: 68'3"

1st Floor: **2,250 sq ft**

2nd Floor: **663 sq ft**

Living Area: **2,913 sq ft**

Bonus Room: **351 sq ft**

Exterior Walls: 2x6

Foundation: Slab

Price Code: **C3**

REAR ELEVATION

© THE SATER DESIGN COLLECTION, INC.

Santa Trinita

A recessed masonry entry echoes the shape of stately turrets and provides both shade and shelter. The front of the home features an arrangement of formal spaces intended for dining and entertaining. To the rear of the plan, the leisure room opens from the kitchen, which is geared for crowd-sized events or family movie nights. A gallery hall runs the width of the plan, linking a cluster of secondary bedrooms and the master suite to the public zone.

4 Bedroom

3-1/2 Bath

Width: 68'8"

Depth: 91'8"

Living Area: **3,497 sq ft**

Exterior Walls: 2x6

Foundation: Slab

Price Code: **C4**

Floor plan labels:

- **Sitting Area** 9'-8" x 7'-6" 10'-0" Clg.
- **Lanai** 25'-0" x 14'-0" 10'-0" Clg.
- **Leisure Room** 18'-2" x 22'-8" 10'-0" to 11'-4" Stepped Clg.
- **Guest Bath**
- Linen
- **Guest Suite** 13'-0" x 13'-0" 10'-0" Clg.
- WIC WIC
- **Nook** 10'-0" Clg.
- **Master Suite** 13'-8" x 17'-3" 10'-0" to 11'-0" Stepped Clg.
- **Pwdr** 10'-0" Clg.
- Built-Ins
- **Living Room** 16'-8" x 16'-6" 12'-0" to 13'-4" Stepped Clg.
- Fireplace
- Built-Ins
- **Kitchen** 15'-4" x 15'-4" 10'-0" to 11'-0" Stepped Clg.
- Pantry
- **Bedroom 2** 13'-0" x 12'-8" 10'-0" Clg.
- **Bath** 10'-0" Clg.
- WIC
- **M. Foyer** 10'-0" Clg.
- **Study** 11'-4" x 14'-2" 13'-0" to 14'-4" Stepped Clg.
- Linen
- **Foyer** 13'-4" Clg.
- **Dining Room** 11'-4" x 13'-6" 14'-0" to 15'-4" Stepped Clg.
- Family Valet
- **Bedroom 1** 12'-2" x 14'-10" 10'-0" Clg.
- WIC
- **M. Bath** 10'-0" Clg.
- Make-Up Area
- Whirlpool
- Walk-In Shower
- **Entry** Beamed Clg.
- Linen
- **Utility** 5'-4" x 8'-4" 10'-0" Clg.
- **Privacy Garden**
- **Garage** 22'-0" x 31'-6" 10'-0" Clg.
- © THE SATER DESIGN COLLECTION, INC.

REAR ELEVATION

© THE SATER DESIGN COLLECTION, INC.

Alessandra

Well-defined formal rooms designed for planned events offer both intimacy and grandeur, while the casual zone provides a relaxing lose-the-shoes atmosphere. Double doors lead from the stair hall to a quiet study, which shares a through-fireplace with the living room and opens to the veranda. On the upper level, a balcony hall benefits from windows to the front and rear of the plan, connecting secondary and guest quarters that boast private decks.

4 Bedroom

3-1/2 Bath

Width: 85'0"

Depth: 76'2"

1st Floor: **2,858 sq ft**

2nd Floor: **1,103 sq ft**

Living Area: **3,961 sq ft**

Exterior Walls: 2x6

Foundation: Slab or Optional Basement

Price Code: **L1**

2ND FLOOR

1ST FLOOR

REAR ELEVATION

© THE SATER DESIGN COLLECTION, INC.

Chadbryne

Old World flair accents this Tuscan design both inside and out. Stately columns distinguish the outline of the front portico and define the dining room. Inside, columns frame the living areas. The curved staircase leads to the secondary bedrooms. The guest suite has a full bath and a walk-in closet. The loft has a built-in computer desk and overlooks the great room below.

4 Bedroom

3-1/2 Bath

Width: 91'0"

Depth: 52'8"

1st Floor: **2,219 sq ft**

2nd Floor: **1,085 sq ft**

Living Area: **3,304 sq ft**

Bonus Room: **404 sq ft**

Exterior Walls: 2x6

Foundation: Slab or Optional Basement

Price Code: **C4**

1st Floor

Veranda
37'-2" x 12'-8"
12'-0" Clg.

Outdoor Grille

Breakfast
13'-0" x 9'-0"
9'-4" to 10'-0"
Beamed Clg.

Built-Ins

Kitchen
14'-6" x 10'-6"
9'-4" to 10'-0"
Beamed Clg.

Great Room
21'-0" x 17'-2"
Open to Above

Fireplace

Entertainment Center

©THE SATER DESIGN COLLECTION, INC.

Garage
23'-0" x 24'-0"
10'-2" Clg.

Master Suite
14'-8" x 17'-0"
12'-0" to 13'-0"
Tray Clg.

WIC

Art Niche

Storage

Dining
13'-0" x 12'-10"
9'-0" to 10'-0"
Stepped Clg.

Foyer
9'-4" to 10'-0"
Stepped Clg.

Pantry
8'-8" Clg.

Utility
9'-0" x 6'-4"
8'-0" Clg.

Up

Dn

Master Bath
11'-0" Clg.

Whirlpool

Walk-In Shower

Powder Bath
9'-4" Clg.

Study/Office
13'-0" x 13'-8"
9'-4" to 10'-0"
Beamed Clg.

Portico
10'-0" Clg.

1ST FLOOR

2nd Floor

©THE SATER DESIGN COLLECTION, INC.

Open to Below
21'-0" to 21'-8"
Coffered Clg.

Bedroom 2
13'-0" x 12'-0"
9'-0" Clg.

WIC

WIC

Dn

Bonus Bath
10'-2" Clg.

Bonus Room
13'-8" x 14'-0"
Vault to 10'-2" Clg.

Walk-In Shower

Bath 1
9'-0" Clg.

Niche

Walk-In Shower

Bath 2
9'-0" Clg.

Walk-In Shower

WIC

Computer Loft
9'-0" Clg.

Dn

Desk

Bedroom 1
13'-0" x 12'-6"
12'-4" Clg.

2ND FLOOR

WIC

Guest Suite
13'-0" x 11'-8"
9'-0" Clg.

Deck

REAR ELEVATION

© THE SATER DESIGN COLLECTION, INC.

Capucina

An open arrangement of the living room, gallery and formal dining room permits great views of the back property through a two-story bow window. French doors open the leisure room to the outdoors, while the morning bay grants access to a lanai shared with the master suite's private sitting bay. Upstairs, a balcony hall — with views of the foyer and living room — leads to family bedrooms, guest quarters and a bonus room.

4 Bedroom

4-1/2 Bath

Width: 71'6"

Depth: 83'0"

1st Floor: **2,855 sq ft**

2nd Floor: **1,156 sq ft**

Living Area: **4,011 sq ft**

Bonus Room: **371 sq ft**

Exterior Walls: 2x6

Foundation: Slab or Optional Basement

Price Code: **L1**

2ND FLOOR

1ST FLOOR

REAR ELEVATION

© THE SATER DESIGN COLLECTION, INC.

© THE SATER DESIGN COLLECTION, INC.

1ST FLOOR

Veranda
10'-0" x 18'-6"
10'-8" Clg.

Garage
25'-0" x 22'-0"
12'-0" Clg.

Outdoor Kitchen

Veranda
34'-0" x 13'-8"
14'-8" Clg.

Master Suite
13'-0" x 16'-10"
10'-8" to 12'-8"
Stepped Clg.

Nook
13'-0" x 10'-10"
10'-0" to 10'-8"
Stepped Clg.

Mud Room
7'-8" x 8'-4"
10'-8" Clg.

Built-Ins

Great Room
19'-6" x 15'-3"
Open to Above

Fireplace

Kitchen
13'-6" x 13'-4"
10'-0" to 10'-8"
Stepped Clg.

Utility
10'-8" Clg.

Built-Ins

Master Foyer

WIC

Pantry

Master Bath
10'-8" Clg.

Art Niche

Whirlpool

Walk-In Shower

WIC

Foyer
10'-8" Clg.

Gallery
10'-8" Clg.

Pwdr

Up

Friends' Entry
10'-8" Clg.

Study
13'-0" x 14'-2"
10'-0" to 10'-8"
Stepped Clg.

Portico
10'-8" Clg.

Dining Room
13'-0" x 13'-10"
10'-2" to 10'-8"
Coffered Clg.

2ND FLOOR

Guest Deck
10'-0" x 18'-6"

Guest Suite
19'-2" x 13'-0"
9'-0" to 10'-0"
Tray Clg.

Open to Below
21'-4" to 22'-0"
Coffered Clg.

Built-In

Guest Bath

Walk-In Shower

W.I.C.

Built-In Bookshelves

Built-In Desk

Stor.

Walk-In Shower

Bath 2

WIC

Loft
9'-4" to 10'-0"
Stepped Clg.

Dn

Bath 1
9'-4" Clg.

Bedroom 2
13'-0" x 13'-10"
12'-4" Clg.

Sun Porch
9'-4" Clg.

Bedroom 1
13'-0" x 13'-10"
9'-4" Clg.

© THE SATER DESIGN COLLECTION, INC.

Vienna

With lovely stonework and columns on both levels of the front elevation, this home exudes a sturdy and stately atmosphere. The various beamed, stepped and coffered ceilings add their own touches of ornate comfort to the interior. The second-story guest suite features its own private deck accessible through French doors.

4 Bedroom

4-1/2 Bath

Width: 80'0"

Depth: 63'8"

1st Floor: **2,232 sq ft**

2nd Floor: **1,245 sq ft**

Living Area: **3,477 sq ft**

Exterior Walls: 2x6

Foundation: Slab or Optional Basement

Price Code: **L1**

REAR ELEVATION

© THE SATER DESIGN COLLECTION, INC.

Royal Palm

Triple arches — in the entryway and windows to the right of the plan — create a commanding presence for this two-story Mediterranean home. A floor plan with an easy flow is highlighted by a living room that has disappearing corner-pocket doors to the lanai.

3 Bedroom

2-1/2 Bath

Width: 65'0"

Depth: 85'4"

Living Area: **2,823 sq ft**

Exterior Walls: 8" CBS

Foundation: Slab

Price Code: **C3**

Leisure Room
16'-10" x 17'-3"
10'-0" Flat Clg.

Entertainment Center

Kitchen
10'-0" Flat

Bedroom
10'-8" x 13'-4"
10'-0" Flat

Bath

Bedroom
10'-8" x 13'-4"
10'-0" Flat

©THE SATER DESIGN
COLLECTION, INC.

Garage
21'-8" x 21'-8"
11'-6" Flat Ceiling

Pantry

Closet

Closet

Closet

Nook
10'-0" Flat

Powder
Bath

Dining Room
12'-2" x 14'-0"
13'/14' Step Clg.

Utility
5'-8" x 9'-6"
10'-0" Flat Clg.

Living Room
15'-4" x 15'-4"
13'/14' Step Clg.

Foyer

Entry

Lanai
10'-0" Flat Clg.

Study
10'-2" x 16'-2"
13'/14' Step Clg.

Gallery

Master Suite
15'-10" x 20'-0"
10'/11' Step Clg.

Master Bath

W.I.C.

Master Garden

REAR ELEVATION

© THE SATER DESIGN COLLECTION, INC.

Plantation Pine

This Old World-style, Italianate home only hints at the unique floor plan that awaits to fulfill every need. Off the master suite is an exercise room and a study with a coffered ceiling and built-in cabinetry. The other wing of the house has a bonus room, computer center and an optional detached guest suite just off the leisure room.

4 or 5 Bedroom

5 Bath

Width: 88'0"

Depth: 133'0"

Guest Suite: **333 sq ft**

Living Area: **4,281 sq ft**

Exterior Walls: 8" CBS

Foundation: Slab

Price Code: **L2**

Floor Plan

Guest Suite
12'-4" x 16'-0"

WIC

Bath 4
Walk-In Shower

Lanai
12'-0" Clg.

Leisure
22'-0" x 22'-0"
12'-0"-14'-0"
Stepped Clg.

Fireplace

Outdoor Kitchen

Enter. Center

Nook
12'-0" Clg.

Guest 1
12'-0" x 16'-0"
10'-0" Clg.

Lanai
45'-0" x 9'-0"
10'-0" Clg.

Sitting

Master Suite
25'-0" x 15'-0"
10'-0"-12'-0"
Stepped Ceiling

Study
18'-8" x 11'-7"
13'-0"-15'-0"
Coffered Ceiling

Living Room
17'-0" x 15'-3"
14'-0"-15'-0"
Stepped Ceiling

Dining
11'-2" x 15'-8"
14'-0"-15'-0"
Stepped Ceiling

Kitchen
17'-2" x 8'-4"

10'-0"-12'-0"
Stepped Clg.

Pantry

Arch

Walk-In Shower

Bath 1

WIC

Bath 2

Tub

Arch

Gallery
12'-0" Clg.

Personal Valet

WIC

Art Niche

Foyer
14'-0-15'-0"
Stepped Clg.

Art Niche

Gallery

Art Niche

Master Bath
10'-0"-11'-0"
Stepped Ceiling

Walk-In Shower

WIC

Exercise
10'-0" x 13'-4"
12'-0" Clg.

Entry

Bath 3
10'-0" Clg.

Computer Center

Guest 2
12'-0" x 13'-0"
10'-0" Clg.

Whirlpool

Private Garden

Bonus Room
16'-8" x 17'-8"
Tray Clg.

Storage

DryAir Cabinet

Studio
10'-0" Clg.

Sink Spa

Iron Station

Duct W/D

Garage
23'-2" x 40'-1"
12'-0" Clg.

©THE SATER DESIGN COLLECTION, INC.

Port Royal Way

A truly dramatic, elegant exterior only gives a hint of the captivating design and wonderful flow of this estate home. As beautiful from the rear as from the front, this home features a spectacular blend of arch-top windows, French doors and balusters. The double-door entry leads to the grand foyer. Columns and archways grace the view through the formal living room. A two-story ceiling, warming fireplace and three pairs of French doors add to the drama.

5 Bedroom

6-1/2 Bath

Width: 98'0"

Depth: 103'8"

1st Floor: **4,760 sq ft**

2nd Floor: **1,552 sq ft**

Living Area: **6,312 sq ft**

Exterior Walls: 8" CBS

Foundation: Slab

Price Code: **L4**

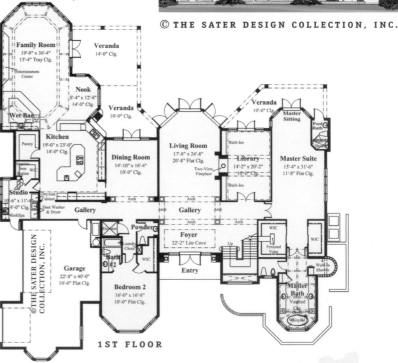

REAR ELEVATION

© THE SATER DESIGN COLLECTION, INC.

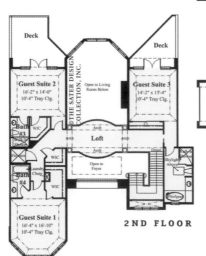

1ST FLOOR

2ND FLOOR

REAR ELEVATION

© THE SATER DESIGN COLLECTION, INC.

Fiddler's Creek

Through the grand foyer the two-story living room features bay glass windows and custom doors. A double-sided fireplace is shared with the study. Across from the study, a windowed turret surrounds the spiral staircase. High ceilings, oversized rooms and elegant façade make this home a timeless choice.

2ND FLOOR

©THE SATER DESIGN COLLECTION, INC.

WIC · Deck · Deck

Bedroom 3
12'-10" x 15'-2"
8'-8" Ceiling

Guest Suite
11'-0" x 19'-8"
8'-8" Ceiling

Open to Below

Bath 2 · WIC · Bath 3 · Linen · WIC

Balcony
8'-8" Ceiling

Open to Below

Bedroom 2
12'-10" x 15'-5"
8'-8" Ceiling

1ST FLOOR

Veranda
28'-0" x 11'-6"
12'-6" Clg.

Leisure Room
20'-8" x 19'-1"
11'-0" to 12'-0"
Coffered Clg.
Built-Ins · Fireplace · Built-Ins · SinkSpa

Duet Washer & Dryer · DryAire Cabinet

Nook
7'-6" x 9'-0"
9'-6" to 10'-0"
Stepped Clg.

Pass-Thru

Veranda
34'-9" x 12'-4"
20'-0" Clg.

Master Suite
14'-10" x 20'-6"
15'-0" to 16'-0"
Stepped Clg.

Kitchen
13'-2" x 20'-0"
9'-6" to 10'-0"
Stepped Clg.
Pantry

Living Room
16'-0" x 14'-4"
Open to Above

2 Sided Fireplace

Study
11'-2" x 12'-8"
10'-0" Clg.

WIC · Personal Valet · WIC

Studio
11'-6" x 8'-8"
Cl.

Optional Impress Iron Center

Art Niche · Art Niche

Gallery
10'-0" Clg.

Bench

Garage
21'-6" x 35'-2"
10'-0" Clg.

Powder Bath

Grand Foyer
Open to Above

Up · Walk-in Shower

Dining
12'-10" x 15'-11"
10'-0" Clg.

Entry

Master Bath
0'-0" Clg.
Whirlpool

©THE SATER DESIGN COLLECTION, INC.

4 Bedroom

3-1/2 Bath

Width: 85'0"

Depth: 76'2"

1st Floor: **2,841 sq ft**

2nd Floor: **1,052 sq ft**

Living Area: **3,893 sq ft**

Exterior Walls: 2x6

Foundation: Slab or Optional Basement

Price Code: **L1**

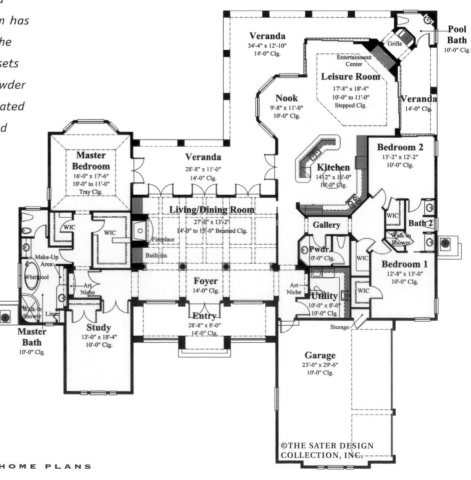

Shiloh

Inspired by the Southwest, this adobe home has a wonderful layout. The open living and dining room has a wood-burning fireplace and a beamed ceiling. The updated bedrooms are oversized, with walk-in closets and an adjoining bath. A conveniently located powder bath serves guests inside, and another bath is located off the patio. The generous leisure room, nook and kitchen allow plenty of space to entertain.

3 Bedroom + Study

2 Full, 2 Half Baths

Width: 84'0"

Depth: 92'0"

Living Area: **3,353 sq ft**

Exterior Walls: 2x6

Foundation: Slab

Price Code: **C4**

REAR ELEVATION

© THE SATER DESIGN COLLECTION, INC.

Sonora

A dramatic dining room opens to the right. Just ahead, the living room is an inviting place to relax by the fireplace. A unique kitchen supports gourmet meals, or a quick snack enjoyed in the sunny nook. An entertainment center separates the leisure and game rooms. The rear guest suite offers a private bath and access to a veranda, featuring an outdoor grille. For the ultimate in luxury, the master suite is peerless: a light-filled sitting area, angled bedroom and indulgent bath.

4 or 5 Bedrooms

3-1/2 Bath

Width: 80'0"

Depth: 107'8"

Living Area: **3,790 sq ft**

Exterior Walls: 2x6

Foundation: Slab

Price Code: **L1**

© THE SATER DESIGN COLLECTION, INC.

REAR ELEVATION

© THE SATER DESIGN COLLECTION, INC.

Echo Canyon

A porte-cochere is the first touch of class that draws you in and leads you through the sophisticated comfort of this rambling, one-story plan. The formal area is immediately inside the front entry and divides the master wing from the family area and secondary bedrooms. A huge verandah runs along the entire rear elevation and is accessible from nearly every room in the house. The master suite boasts its own private garden.

3 Bedroom

3-1/2 Bath

Width: 121'5"

Depth: 99'6"

Living Area: **3,384 sq ft**

Exterior Walls: 2x6

Foundation: Slab

Price Code: **C4**

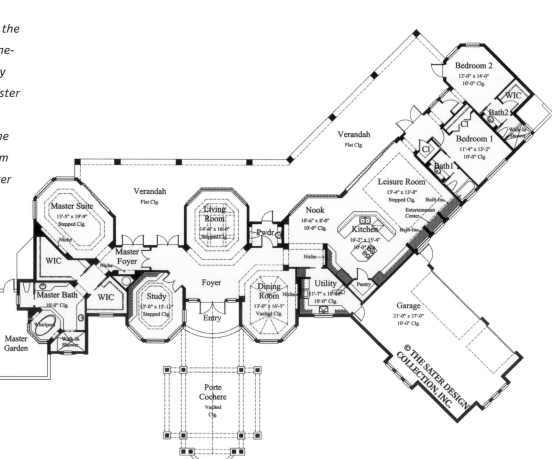

REAR ELEVATION

© THE SATER DESIGN COLLECTION, INC.

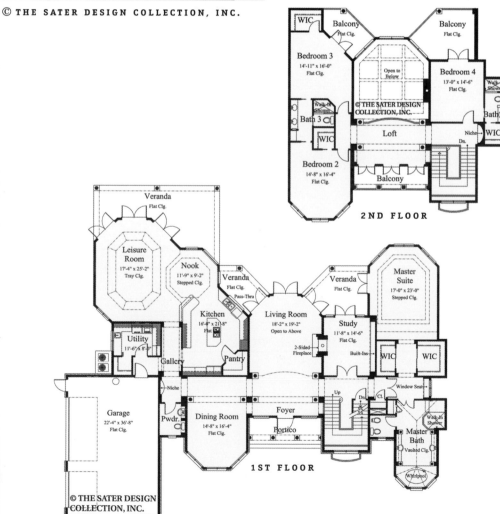

Flagstone Ridge

The dramatic use of stacked stone amidst arch-top windows gives this home a dignified and warm façade. A front portico under triple arches leads to the foyer and living room, where three pair of French doors open to the veranda and breathtaking views. French doors also lead outside from the study, master suite and oversized leisure room. A second-floor loft views the living room and connects to three upstairs bedrooms.

4 Bedroom

4-1/2 Bath

Width: 95'0"

Depth: 84'8"

1st Floor: **3,556 sq ft**

2nd Floor: **1,253 sq ft**

Living Area: **4,809 sq ft**

Exterior Walls: 2x6

Foundation: Slab

Price Code: **L2**

Lochwood Drive

Brendan Cove

PLAN 6675

5 Bed / 3 Bath

Living Area: **3,285 sq ft**

Width: 66'0" / Depth: 80'6"

Exterior Walls: 8" CBS

Foundation: Slab

Price Code: **C4**

REAR ELEVATION

© THE SATER DESIGN COLLECTION, INC.

PLAN 6740

4 Bed / 5 Bath

Living Area: **4,633 sq ft**

Width: 76'8" / Depth: 113'0"

Exterior Walls: 8" CBS

Foundation: Slab

Price Code: **L2**

REAR ELEVATION

© THE SATER DESIGN COLLECTION, INC.

1st Floor: 2,747 sq ft

2nd Floor: 538 sq ft

1st Floor: 3,670 sq ft

2nd Floor: 963 sq ft

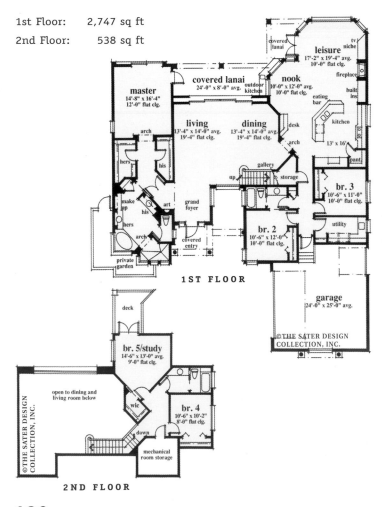

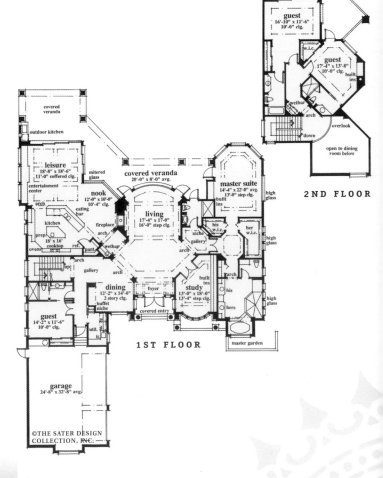

Della Porta

PLAN 8007

3 Bed / 3-1/2 Bath

Living Area: **3,640 sq ft**

Width: 106'4" / Depth: 102'4"

Exterior Walls: 2x6

Foundation:
Slab or Optional Basement

Price Code: **L 1**

Vasari

PLAN 8025

5 Bed / 5-1/2 Bath

Living Area: **4,160 sq ft**

Width: 58'0" / Depth: 65'0"

Exterior Walls: 2x6

Foundation:
Slab or Optional Basement

Price Code: **L 2**

1st Floor: 1,995 sq ft
2nd Floor: 2,165 sq ft

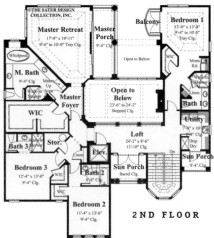

2ND FLOOR

1ST FLOOR

Trevi

Teodora

PLAN 8065

4 Bed / 3-1/2 Bath

Living Area: **4,837 sq ft**

Width: 95'0" / Depth: 84'0"

Exterior Walls: 2x6

Foundation: Basement

Price Code: **L2**

REAR ELEVATION

© THE Sater DESIGN COLLECTION, INC.

1st Floor: 3,581 sq ft

2nd Floor: 1,256 sq ft

PLAN 8066

5 Bed / 3-1/2 Bath

Living Area: **3,993 sq ft**

Width: 80'0" / Depth: 104'0"

Exterior Walls: 8" CBS

Foundation: Slab

Price Code: **L 1**

REAR ELEVATION

© THE Sater DESIGN COLLECTION, INC.

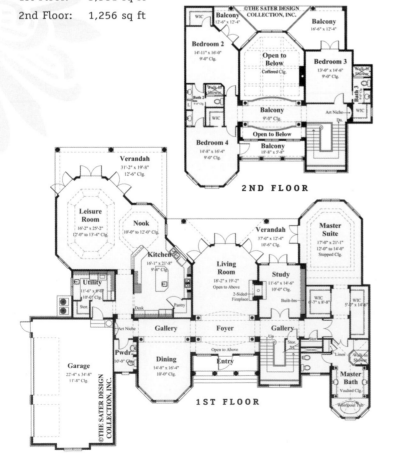

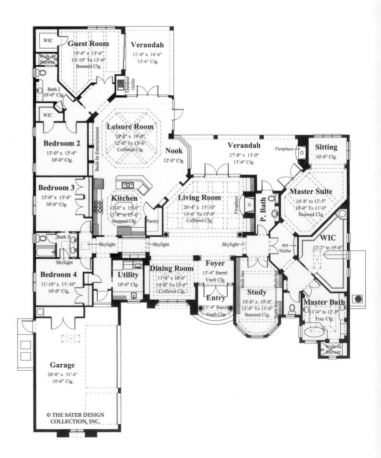

Simone

PLAN 8059

4 Bed / 3-1/2 Bath

Living Area: **3,231 sq ft**

Width: 67'0" / Depth: 91'8"

Exterior Walls: 2x6 or 8" CBS

Foundation: Slab

Price Code: **C4**

REAR ELEVATION

© THE SATER DESIGN COLLECTION, INC.

Massimo

PLAN 8057

5 Bed / 4-1/2 Bath

Living Area: **4,398 sq ft**

Width: 69'4" / Depth: 95'4"

Exterior Walls: 2x6

Foundation:
Slab or Optional Basement

Price Code: **L2**

REAR ELEVATION

© THE SATER DESIGN COLLECTION, INC.

1st Floor: 2,920 sq ft

2nd Floor: 1,478 sq ft

Mediterranean Index | PLANS LISTED BY SQUARE FOOTAGE LARGEST TO SMALLEST

PLAN NAME	PLAN #	PRICE CODE	PAGE	SQ. FT.
Alamosa	6940	PSE5	68	8,088
Napier	6926	PSE5	154	6,855
Huntington Lakes	6900	PSE5	136	6,770
Casa Bellisima	6935	PSE5	36	6,524
Port Royal Way	6635	L4	176	6,312
Fiorentino	6910	PSE5	50	6,273
Lindley	6930	PSE5	44	6,011
Sterling Oaks	6914	PSE5	90	5,816
Dauphino	6933	PSE5	84	5,804
Ristano	6939	PSE5	56	5,564
Sancho	6947	PSE5	30	5,335
Marrakesh	6942	PSE5	22	5,109
Saraceno	6929	PSE5	96	5,013
La Ventana	6925	PSE5	151	5,009
Gambier Court	6948	PSE5	100	4,951
Trevi	8065	L2	184	4,837
Flagstone Ridge	6765	L2	181	4,809
Sherbrooke	6742	PSE5	132	4,771
Brendan Cove	6740	L2	182	4,633
Cataldi	6946	PSE5	78	4,588
Autumn Woods	6753	PSE5	108	4,534
Cantadora	6949	PSE5	104	4,528
Martinique	6932	PSE5	62	4,492
Porto Velho	6950	PSE5	72	4,492
Massimo	8057	L2	185	4,398
Plantation Pine	6735	L2	175	4,281
Monticello	6907	PSE5	140	4,255
Vasari	8025	L2	183	4,160
La Reina	8046	L2	165	4,151
Capucina	8010	L1	172	4,011
Monterrey Lane	6672	PSE5	124	4,009
Teodora	8066	L1	184	3,993
Verrado	6918	L1	161	3,991

Mediterranean Index

PLAN NAME	PLAN #	PRICE CODE	PAGE	SQ. FT.
Alessandra	8003	L1	170	3,945
Laparelli	8035	L1	160	3,942
Broadmoor Walk	6641	L1	148	3,896
Fiddler's Creek	6746	L1	177	3,893
Starwood	6911	PSE5	144	3,877
Grimaldi Court	6783	PSE5	116	3,817
Sonora	6764	L1	179	3,790
Salina	8043	L1	164	3,743
Della Porta	8007	L1	183	3,640
Corsini	8049	L1	159	3,578
Vienna	8020	L1	173	3,501
Martelli	8061	C4	163	3,497
Santa Trinita	8063	C4	169	3,497
Salcito	6787	C4	152	3,473
Echo Canyon	6766	C4	180	3,384
Shiloh	6763	C4	178	3,353
Bellini	8042	C4	162	3,351
Chadbryne	8004	C4	171	3,304
Lochwood Drive	6675	C4	182	3,285
Caprina	8052	C4	167	3,271
Simone	8059	C4	185	3,231
Rosario	6784	C4	155	3,184
Porta Rossa	8058	C4	166	3,105
Ferretti	6786	C4	153	3,031
Raphaello	8037	C3	168	2,913
Deauville	6778	PSE5	128	2,908
Kinsey	6756	C3	112	2,907
Royal Palm	6727	C3	174	2,823
Bartolini	8022	C3	158	2,736
Esperane	6759	C3	157	2,654
La Posada	6785	C3	156	2,554
Toscana	6758	C2	120	2,329

Blueprints | WHAT'S IN A SET?

Each set of plans is a collection of drawings that show how your house is to be built. The actual number of pages may vary, but most plan packages include the following:

A-1 COVER SHEET/INDEX & SITE PLAN

An Artist's Rendering of the exterior of the house shows you approximately how the house will look when built and landscaped. The Index is a list of the sheets included and page numbers for easy reference. The Site Plan is a scaled drawing of the house to help determine the placement of the home on a building site.

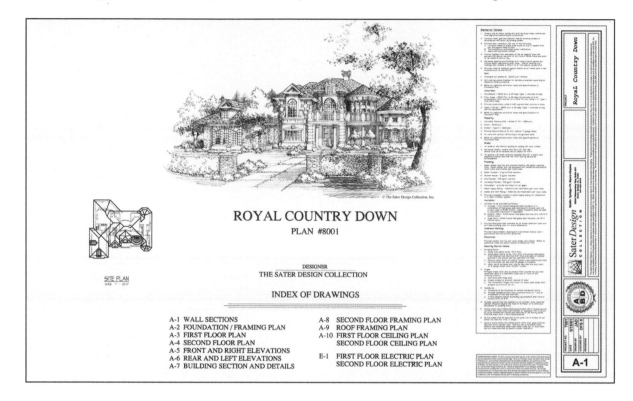

A-2 WALL SECTION / NOTES

This sheet shows details of the house from the roof to the foundation. This section specifies the home's construction, insulation, flooring and roofing details.

A-3 FOUNDATION PLAN

This sheet gives the foundation layout, including support walls, excavated and unexcavated areas, if any, and foundation notes. If the foundation is monolithic slab rather than basement, the plan shows footing and details.

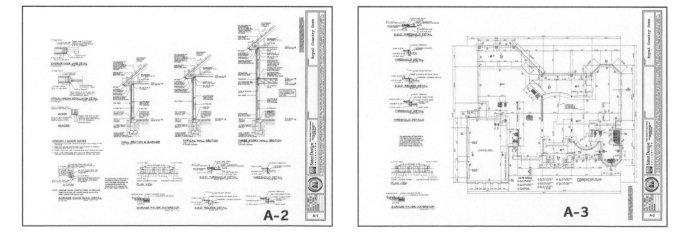

A-4 DETAILED FLOOR PLANS

These plans show the layout of each floor of the house. Rooms and interior spaces are carefully dimensioned and keys are given for cross-section details provided later in the plans, as well as window and door size callouts. These plans also show the location of kitchen appliances and bathroom fixtures, etc.

A-5 CEILING PLAN

Sater ceiling treatments are typically very detailed. This plan shows ceiling layout and extensive details.

A-6 ROOF PLAN

Overall layout and necessary details for roof construction are provided. If trusses are used, we suggest using a local truss manufacturer to design trusses to comply with your local codes and regulations.

A-7 EXTERIOR ELEVATIONS

Included are front, rear, left and right sides of the house. Exterior materials, details and measurements are also given.

A-8 CROSS SECTION & DETAILS

Important changes in floor, ceiling and roof heights or the relationship of one level to another are called out. Also shown, when applicable, are exterior details such as railing and banding.

A-9 INTERIOR ELEVATIONS

These plans show the specific details and design of cabinets, utility rooms, fireplaces, bookcases, built-in units and other special interior features, depending on the nature and complexity of the item.

A-10 SECOND FLOOR FRAMING

This sheet shows directional spacing for floor trusses, beam locations and load-bearing conditions, if any.

E-1 ELECTRICAL PLAN

This sheet shows wiring and the suggested locations for switches, fixtures and outlets.

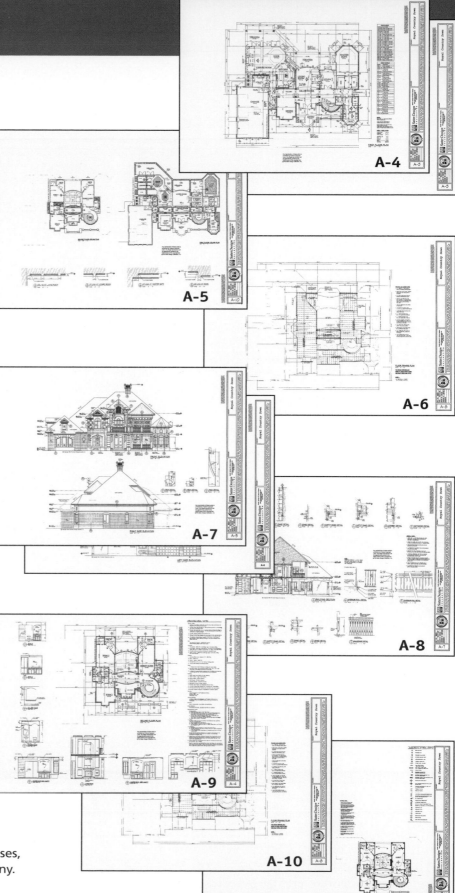

QUICK TURNAROUND

Because you are placing your order directly, we can ship plans to you quickly. If your order is placed before noon EST, we can usually have your plans to you the next business day. Some restrictions may apply. We cannot ship to a post office box; please provide a physical street address.

OUR EXCHANGE POLICY

Since our blueprints are printed especially for you at the time you place your order, we cannot accept any returns. If, for some reason, you find that the plan that you purchased does not meet your needs, then you may exchange that plan for another plan in our collection. We allow you sixty days from the time of purchase to make an exchange. At the time of the exchange, you will be charged a processing fee of 20% of the total amount of the original order, plus the difference in price between the plans (if applicable) and the cost to ship the new plans to you. Vellums cannot be exchanged. All sets must be approved and authorization given before the exchange can take place. Please call our customer service department if you have any questions.

LOCAL BUILDING CODES AND ZONING REQUIREMENTS

Our plans are designed to meet or exceed national building standards. Because of the great differences in geography and climate, each state, county and municipality has its own building codes and zoning requirements. Your plan may need to be modified to comply with local requirements regarding snow loads, energy codes, soil and seismic conditions and a wide range of other matters. Prior to using plans ordered from us, we strongly advise that you consult a local building official.

ARCHITECTURE AND ENGINEERING SEALS

Some cities and states are now requiring that a licensed architect or engineer review and approve any set of building documents prior to construction. This is due to concerns over energy costs, safety, structural integrity and other factors. Prior to applying for a building permit or the start of actual construction, we strongly advise that you consult your local building official who can tell you if such a review is required.

DISCLAIMER

We have put substantial care and effort into the creation of our blueprints. We authorize the use of our blueprints on the express condition that you strictly comply with all local building codes, zoning requirements and other applicable laws, regulations and ordinances. However, because we cannot provide on-site consultation, supervision or control over actual construction, and because of the great variance in local building requirements, building practices and soil, seismic, weather and other conditions, WE CANNOT MAKE ANY WARRANTY, EXPRESS OR IMPLIED, WITH RESPECT TO THE CONTENT OR USE OF OUR BLUEPRINTS OR VELLUMS, INCLUDING BUT NOT LIMITED TO ANY WARRANTY OF MERCHANTABILITY OR OF FITNESS FOR A PARTICULAR PURPOSE. Please Note: Floor plans in this book are not construction documents and are subject to change. Renderings are artist's concept only.

HOW MANY SETS OF PRINTS WILL YOU NEED?

We offer a single set of prints so that you can study and plan your dream home in detail. However, you cannot build from this package. One set of blueprints is marked "NOT FOR CONSTRUCTION." If you are planning to obtain estimates from a contractor or subcontractor, or if you are planning to build immediately, you will need more sets. Because additional sets are less expensive, make sure you order enough to satisfy all your requirements. Sometimes changes are needed to a plan; in that case, we offer vellums that are reproducible and erasable so changes can be made directly to the plans. Vellums are the only set that can be reproduced; it is illegal to copy blueprints. The checklist below will help you determine how many sets are needed.

Plan Checklist

_____ **Owner** (one for notes, one for file)

_____ **Builder** (generally requires at least three sets; one as a legal document, one for inspections and at least one to give subcontractors)

_____ **Local Building Department** (often requires two sets)

_____ **Mortgage Lender** (usually one set for a conventional loan; three sets for FHA or VA loans)

_____ **Total Number of Sets**

IGNORING COPYRIGHT LAWS CAN BE A
$1,000,000 mistake!

Recent changes in the US copyright laws allow for statutory penalties of up to $150,000 per incident for copyright infringement involving any of the copyrighted plans found in this publication. The law can be confusing. So, for your own protection, take the time to understand what you cannot do when it comes to home plans.

WHAT YOU CAN'T DO!

YOU CANNOT DUPLICATE HOME PLANS

YOU CANNOT COPY ANY PART OF A HOME PLAN TO CREATE ANOTHER

YOU CANNOT BUILD A HOME WITHOUT BUYING A BLUEPRINT OR LICENSE

SATER DESIGN COLLECTION, INC.

25241 Elementary Way, Suite 201
Bonita Springs, FL 34135

1-800-718-7526

www.saterdesign.com

sales@saterdesign.com

ADDITIONAL ITEMS

11x17 Color Rendering Front Perspective* $100.00
Material List $75.00
Additional Blueprints (per set) $65.00
Reverse Mirror-Image Blueprints $50.00

*Call for availability. Special orders may require additional fees.

POSTAGE AND HANDLING

Overnight $52.00
2nd Day $42.00
Ground $32.00
Saturday $72.00

For shipping international, please call for a quote.

BLUEPRINT PRICE SCHEDULE*

	5 SETS	8 SETS	VELLUM
C1	$725	$785	$970
C2	$770	$830	$1040
C3	$820	$890	$1120
C4	$875	$940	$1200
L1	$1015	$1100	$1365
L2	$1090	$1185	$1490
L3	$1210	$1300	$1655
L4	$1325	$1420	$1820
PSE5	Call for pricing		

* Prices subject to change without notice

Order Form

PLAN NUMBER _____

☐ 5-set building package . . . . $_____
☐ 8-set building package . . . . $_____
☐ 1-set of reproducible vellums . . . . $_____

____ Additional Identical Blueprints @ $65 each $_____
____ Reverse Mirror-Image Blueprints @ $50 fee $_____

Sub-Total $_____
Shipping and Handling $_____
Sales Tax (FL Res.) 6% $_____

TOTAL $_____

Check one: ☐ Visa ☐ MasterCard

Credit Card Number _____

Expiration Date _____

Signature _____

Name _____

Company _____

Street _____

City _____ State_____ Zip_____

Daytime Telephone Number (_____) _____

Check one:

☐ Consumer ☐ Builder ☐ Developer

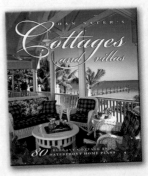